# Are you asking yourself these questions?

- Can God forgive me for what I did (or am doing)?
- How can I forgive myself?
- What can I do about the depression I feel?
- How can I rid myself of plaguing memories?
- Can I be useful to God again after what I've done?
- How do I get out of an immoral relationship?
- Can I ever have a godly relationship with someone of the opposite sex?

Let Dick Purnell give you some realistic, practical steps you can take that will help you face your sexual regrets and show you how to handle them. You will discover how to walk confidently beyond those regrets and toward healthy relationships with the opposite sex.

# FREE
# TO LOVE
# AGAIN

## DICK PURNELL

**THOMAS NELSON PUBLISHERS**
Nashville

Published in Nashville, Tennessee, by Thomas Nelson, Inc.,
Publishers, and distributed in Canada by Word Communica-
tions, Ltd., Richmond, British Columbia, and in the United
Kingdom by Word (UK), Ltd., Milton Keynes, England.

Unless otherwise indicated, Scripture quotations are from the
HOLY BIBLE, NEW INTERNATIONAL VERSION ®. Copy-
right © 1973, 1978, 1984 by International Bible Society. Used
by permission of Zondervan Bible Publishing House. All rights
reserved.

The "NIV" and "New International Version" trademarks are
registered in the United States Patent and Trademark Office by
International Bible Society. Use of either trademark requires
the permission of International Bible Society.

Scripture quotations designated KJV are from The Holy Bible,
KING JAMES VERSION.

**Library of Congress Cataloging-in-Publication Data**
Purnell, Dick.
    Free to love again / Dick Purnell.
        p. cm.
    Reprint. Originally published: San Bernardino, CA: Here's
Life Publishers, c1989.
    Includes bibliographical references.
    ISBN 0-8407-4275-4 (pbk.)
    1. Sex—Religious aspects—Christianity. 2. Christian life—
1960-
    I. Title.
    [BT708.P77 1993]
    241'.66—dc20                                              93-32158
                                                             CIP

Printed in the United States of America
1 2 3 4 5 6 7 8 - 98 97 96 95 94 93

»»»» ¤ «««««

to Herb and Elsie Purnell,
my older brother and his wife.

Through these many years,
you have been to me
a great example of a couple
who deeply love God
and each other.
I love and respect you beyond words.

# »»»» CONTENTS ««««

# »»» ACKNOWLEDGMENTS «««

A book is the result of the efforts of a lot of people besides the author. Without their help, it would not be brought into existence. It is to the following people that I give my deepest thanks and appreciation for assisting me:

**All the men and women** who allowed me to use their life experiences and lessons as illustrations. Even though your names have been changed in this book, you are known to me and to God.

**Tom Lowder, Bonnie Davis, Tina Jacobson** and **Gary Woodson.** In our interactions and discussions you gave me valuable ideas for the original concepts for the book and helped with the basic content of some of the chapters.

**Ed Stewart**. You took my original writings and refined them. This book would still be on the planning board without you.

**Andria Wolfe** and **Ginni Christopher**. Your help in typing, managing our Single Life Resources office, and proofing the manuscript helped me meet my deadlines and finish the book.

**Paula Purnell**. What a great job you did in editing the final copy of the manuscript. My wife, lover, and the mother of my two daughters—I love and appreciate you more each day. God knew what He was doing when He brought us together.

## »»  PART I  ««

## SEXUAL REGRETS

# »»» CHAPTER ONE «««

## A TREASURE CHEST FULL OF HOPE

Brett and Sandra had no idea what the painful long-range effects of their lifestyle before marriage would be. Both had been sexually active before they met. When they fell in love with each other, they generously shared sexual intimacy. They thought they had avoided any negative consequences of their sexual permissiveness. "We are having fun and we love each other," they reasoned. "Besides, we plan to get married."

Five years and two children later, Brett and Sandra are on the verge of divorce. They can't trust each other to be faithful to their marriage vows. When Brett is traveling on business, Sandra imagines him going to bed with other women, and Brett suspects that Sandra is flirting with other men while he's gone.

Premarital sex had seemed free of concerns, but now Brett and Sandra were reaping the dark consequences of mutual distrust, suspicion and sexual regret.

Roger and Lisa were desperate for love. Roger was not thinking of the down side of sexual intimacy when he talked Lisa into going to bed with him, but Lisa became pregnant. Roger was suddenly overcome with remorse by what he had done. He wanted to hide his guilt and fear, and he slid into deep depression. His agony drove him to seek God's forgiveness and healing from the pain.

However, Lisa's pregnancy didn't go away. They talked about abortion, but finally decided against it. They knew that a hasty marriage wasn't the answer either, so they decided to have the baby and give it up for adoption.

Roger wanted to do the right thing. Even though he didn't love Lisa, he stuck with her through the pregnancy and was in the delivery room when she gave birth to a beautiful little boy. In the state where they live, the law requires a 48-hour period between the birth of the infant and the time to give the child over to the adoptive parents. Roger and Lisa had only two days to enjoy their little son before giving him away.

A couple of weeks later I received a photo from Roger. It's the saddest picture I've ever seen. It showed Roger placing his tiny, bundled-up son in the arms of the new adoptive parents. When I read the caption on the back of the photo I wept. It simply read, "Saying goodbye."

My wife Paula and I are the parents of two lovely daughters, and I shudder to imagine the emotional upheaval it would be to have to part with either of them. Yet for Roger and Lisa, the gutwrenching nightmare became a reality. It will take them years to recover from the down side of their fleeting sexual encounter, if they ever do.

The negative consequences affect people of all ages. I found the following handwritten, unsigned note pinned to a high school bulletin board:

*To anyone,*

*I need help to understand what life is all about, to see the way my life should go. Does God forgive me for all my sins? I need to see that I can live the Christian life, that I can change to fit in. I want to live a whole life without always needing a man in my life.*

*And I have a question. Is there someone out there who will want to marry a girl who isn't a virgin? Before you answer, think about this: This girl has had intercourse before. You don't know how many guys she's had intercourse with. How do you know that, after you are married, she won't go out and find someone else? Okay, maybe she said she wouldn't, but if she's had intercourse with other strange guys, why wouldn't she go out and do it again?*

*She is a Christian and knows what she did was wrong, but she can't block out what she did. She isn't pure anymore and never will be. That's the way it is with me. I'm not pure. I will never be pure again. Oh, why did I do what I did? Tell me, if you can, why do people do that kind of thing?*

*Thank you for listening, whoever you are. Please go in peace.*

Can you identify with the inner pain and hopelessness described in these real-life examples? Maybe you have been involved in premarital or extramarital sex, only to be swamped by waves of pain and regret. Or you may not have gotten involved yet, but you are presently in a romantic relationship to the point where you are afraid you will give in to sexual pressure. Moral failure is a scary possibility.

## THAT HELPLESS, HOPELESS FEELING

There's a story in Greek mythology about Zeus, the supreme deity, and the man he created. Zeus was afraid that one day that man would reach out for his throne. He felt tricked by another god who had given man great powers, so Zeus decided to express his anger toward the man by playing a cruel trick on him. He created a beautiful woman named Pandora and gave her to the man. Then the vengeful Zeus also gave Pandora an ornate box, something like a small treasure chest.

"Whatever you do," Zeus instructed Pandora, "don't open the box." Zeus knew that Pandora's curiosity would eventually trigger his vengeance on the man.

At first Pandora had little trouble ignoring the box. As time wore on, though, she began to wonder what was inside. It was such an exquisite box, and Pandora suspected that the contents were as exquisite as the container. A couple of times her curiosity almost got the best of her, but her husband, afraid of Zeus's wrath, stopped her from opening the box.

Finally, while her husband was away on a trip, Pandora could not control her curiosity any longer. She crept to the box and lifted the lid. Suddenly out of the box exploded all the world's troubles and evils—hardship, poverty, old age, sickness, jealousy, vice, passion and distrust. In terror, Pandora realized her mistake and tried to slam the lid shut, but it was too late.

At last all the horrible evils inside the box had been scattered throughout the world to plague mankind. Zeus was delighted. Despondent, Pandora looked into the box. There were no riches or treasures as she had imagined. The only thing left inside Pandora's box was hope! [1]

## LOTS OF GLITTER, LITTLE GOLD

For a large number of people today, sexual intimacy outside marriage is as irresistible as the box was for Pandora. When I say "sexual intimacy outside marriage," I'm referring to the passionate, skin-on-skin closeness which leads to premarital or extramarital sexual intercourse — from steamy one-night stands to casual affairs to long-term, live-in partnerships.

In our culture, sex outside marriage is increasingly alluring because of the free promotion it gets. Our friends give us the juicy details of their spicy encounters. The media dangles products before us which are supposed to transform us into virile and voluptuous your-place-or-mine sex machines.

Television programs, movies, romance novels and magazines glamorize the adventure and beauty of "responsible" sex — and it all looks so safe, so thrilling, so positive, so good, and so much like fun.

Make no mistake: Sexual intimacy within the God-ordained parameters of marriage is wonderful and fulfilling. God created sex, and He designed our bodies with the capacity to enjoy it fully.

Being sexually active outside the marriage bond, though, as glamorous as it may appear, is like opening Pandora's box. It has a down side which people don't know about — and don't want to know about. Once the momentary sexual excitement has ended, the repercussions can be devastating. Out of the box pours mental, emotional and physical anguish — guilt, shame, frustration, loss of respect, distrust. Out of the box pour traumatic experiences — a devastating breakup, an abortion, a hasty marriage, an unwanted child, venereal disease. Lift the lid on sexual intimacy outside marriage and it explodes in your face.

## HELP YOURSELF TO THE HOPE

This book is not written to condemn you or make you feel you're a lost cause. Rather, I want to point you to the bright, warm light at the end of the tunnel. Remember: After her box had spewed out all its evil contents, Pandora still had hope. In the midst of all the negative consequences and feelings from your experience with sexual intimacy, I want you to see the hope offered to you through Christ and through the Scriptures.

This hope is not a superficial wish for your recovery. I'm not telling you to hang on until some day when everything will turn out okay, when you will feel better and your moral dilemma will be resolved, because that won't happen. No, I want to give you some realistic, practical steps you can take now. They will bring you face to face with your sexual regrets, show you how to handle them, and help you walk confidently beyond them and toward healthy, loving relationships with the opposite sex. That *can* happen.

# »»»» CHAPTER TWO ««««

## CLOSING PANDORA'S BOX

When I was about ten years old, a well-known artist came to our church as a guest speaker. He talked about God's Word as he drew beautiful scenes of nature with colored chalk.

One drawing stands out vividly in my memory. The artist sketched a landscape of majestic purple mountains reflected in a serene lake surrounded by evergreens. He filled the large paper with color, and he talked about the perfection and beauty of God's creation. My eyes were wide with wonder as he completed the picture. It was perfect.

Then, while the audience was still admiring his drawing, the artist picked up a large wedge of black chalk and quickly swept it across the paper, leaving an ugly black line right down the middle!

The audience gasped and my mouth dropped open in shock, "He's ruined the picture!"

I almost cried.

Then the artist began to talk about sin. "God's creation was perfect until sin entered the world," he said. "The disobedience of Adam and Eve ruined God's perfect creation just as surely as the black mark has ruined this landscape. Because of sin, our lives are just as scarred as this picture." I suddenly understood — more clearly than ever before — the awful effects of sin.

The artist, still holding the black chalk, began adding something to the ugly mark. "But God has a remedy for sin," he said. I strained to see what he was doing. "God has a way of transforming the ugliness of our sinful lives into something beautiful."

I scarcely breathed as I watched the artist cover the black mark with two or three strokes, making a dark vertical shaft. Then, near the top of the shaft, he drew a horizontal beam across it. He stepped back and I was amazed. The ugly mark on the landscape had turned into the silhouette of a cross planted in the foreground. The picture was hauntingly beautiful again.

"That's what Jesus has done for us through His death on the cross and His resurrection," the artist said. "The ugly marks of sin in our lives have been replaced by the symbol of forgiveness and victory. Jesus Christ can take any situation, no matter how scarred it is, and change it for the better."

## GRABBING FOR HOPE

I often think of that chalk drawing when counseling people who feel scarred by moral failure and sexual regret. They see their lives as permanently ruined, just like the beautiful landscape slashed with black. The emotional tug of war has dragged them through the mud. They feel dirty, damaged, worthless and hopeless.

There is good news, though, for those whose lives are scarred by impurity: The cross of Christ can turn disaster into hope and victory. You can't erase the past — but you don't need to be a victim of it. You can find forgiveness for your past and its pains.

Nor are you chained to your present patterns of behavior which threaten to drag you through the mud again and again. You can stop the process. You can turn this area of your life around. You can replace that hurtful behavior with productive behavior.

Like Pandora, you may feel overwhelmed by a whole box full of troubles and disappointments from your past experiences which have obliterated your hope for the future. Your world has been irreparably harmed.

Yet, even if you feel you have nothing else, you do have hope. You are surviving the pain of the emotional tug of war. You are coming to grips with your responsibility, your part in what has happened. Now it's time to grab the hope that Christ offers through the healing of the cross and the power of the resurrection, and slam the lid down on that box. Start experiencing the change He can make in your life.

## THERE'LL BE SOME CHANGES MADE

Many of the individuals I counsel have big dreams about how they are going to turn their moral failures around through personal determination and discipline. They say, "I blew it before, but it will be different now. I'm going to turn over a new leaf. I'm never again going to behave the same way toward the opposite sex."

This noble-sounding approach reminds me of Benjamin Franklin's famous experiment to change his life by adding thirteen virtues to his behavior. One week he concentrated on virtue number one (patience) and did very well. The next week he concentrated on virtue number two (kindness), but as he did, his patience went out the window! As long as he focused on one virtue he succeeded with it, yet each time he changed his focus, his previous successes fell apart. For seven years he tried to change his life, but he never succeeded. He finally admitted defeat.

That's the way it often is when we try to pull ourselves up by our own bootstraps. Our firm intentions get soft after awhile and eventually peter out. Our New Year's resolutions last until about mid-January, and then we're back where we started.

Some couples determine to change by making new rules for their relationships. "We're setting limits for ourselves now," I've heard them say. "We're not going to do anything beyond kissing." When new rules meet old habits head on, though, the old habits usually win.

Other couples decide they're going to change by praying together. They think that if they huddle together in the apartment to pray, the results will be different from when they huddled together romantically in the same apartment. Prayer should be an important part of every dating relationship—but you would be surprised at the number of couples who confess to me that a date which began with prayer ended up with hot passion. There's more to changing than making a commitment to pray together.

Still other couples attempt to break their patterns of impure behavior by breaking up and finding new partners. They complain, "I just can't control myself when I'm with my date, so I'd better find someone else." Yet they always bring themselves into the next relationship, and their own patterns of behavior have not been changed. Only their date's name is different. They soon discover that they suffer the same old temptations with their new partners.

The problem with changing behavior is that we do not understand where change comes from. In the process of earning my master's degree in counseling from Indiana University, I studied all the popular theories of psychotherapy and counseling. All of them claim that man is inherently good. They contend that, given enough guidance, therapy, drugs, time, etc., anyone is capable of changing himself and his behavior for the better.

I don't believe we are basically good, nor does the Bible support it. Left to ourselves, our selfishness reigns supreme. We are inherently sinful, incomplete and incapable of doing good consistently.

God declared: "The heart is deceitful above all things and beyond cure. Who can understand it?" (Jeremiah 17:9).

Jesus stated, "Apart from me you can do nothing" (John 15:5).

Paul wrote: "Not that we are competent to claim anything for ourselves, but our competence comes from God" (2 Corinthians 3:5).

We may be able to change some superficial things about ourselves, but we are unable to change our sinful nature. God must change us from the inside out.

That is your greatest reason for hope. God *can* change you. God is *willing* to change you. You don't have the power to change yourself, but He has the power to change you. That was the message of hope Paul brought to the Ephesians:

> I pray also that the eyes of your heart may be enlightened in order that you may know the hope to which he has called you, the riches of his glorious inheritance in the saints, and his in-

comparably great power for us who believe. That power is like
the working of his mighty strength, which he exerted in Christ
when he raised him from the dead and seated him at his right
hand in heavenly realms (Ephesians 1:18-20).

The power at God's disposal to free you from your
past and change your life is the same power God used to
raise Christ from the dead. It's His "incomparably great
power" — you can't find anything like it anywhere else!
And He has unleashed His same great power to work in
"us who believe." As with the chalk artist's drawing, the
healing of the cross and the power of the resurrection are
available to transform your mistakes into His master-
piece. Now that's a hope worth grabbing for!

## FROM DESPAIR TO HOPE

If anyone were a candidate for God's power and
hope, it was Susan. If you talked to her today, you would
never guess the horror and heartache of sexual regret
that clouded her past. Susan's story, which she and her
husband told me, exemplifies how God's power can restore a life which was practically ruined through immorality.

As a teenager I lived pretty much apart from
parental supervision. I had a steady boyfriend
and we were sexually active. Like a lot of girls, I
didn't really want sex, I just wanted to be loved.
At the time, sex seemed like the way to get what
I wanted. Instead, I got pregnant when I was 16.

In those days abortions were not talked about,
and they were illegal in most states. So on my
doctor's recommendation, my family sent me to
New York for a quiet abortion. It was a horrible
experience. Even though nobody told me it was
biblically wrong, I knew deep inside I had made a
terrible mistake.

When I got home I suffered from extreme
guilt and severe depression. I lost all interest in

life. My friends noticed the change in me and drifted away. Instead of being one of the most popular girls in school, I became an outcast and a loner. I dated the wrong kinds of guys because I felt unworthy to be seen with anyone better.

I dated one guy through most of my college years and was sexually active during this time. Everyone thought I was a prude, but I lived a lie. It seemed like sex was the only way for me to get the acceptance I craved.

Just before I left college I began dating my roommate's boyfriend Brian behind her back. Shortly after getting involved with Brian, I married him—for all the wrong reasons. I knew as I walked down the aisle to get married that it wasn't right, but I didn't know what else to do. My self-image was so low that I thought having a committed sex partner would resolve my feelings of worthlessness. Of course, it didn't.

Six weeks into the marriage I was miserable and wanted out. I was unfaithful to Brian regularly. When I told him I was having an abortion he thought I wasn't ready for kids yet. In reality, I wanted an abortion because I didn't know who the father was. Soon after the abortion I divorced Brian.

I became a flight attendant and my lifestyle continued to be a moral shambles. One night I had a terrible sexual experience, one I didn't even want to be involved in. I came home afterward and cried out, "Help me, God. Whatever it takes, I'll do it—anything you say. I'll turn my whole life over to you if you'll just help me."

God heard my prayer and, about two years later, I accepted Christ through the witness of another flight attendant I was rooming with at

the time. I immediately realized that I had to
start changing my habits. For example, when I
had a layover during a plane trip, I decided to
stay in my hotel room instead of going down to
the bar with the crew. My friends at work started
calling me names and making fun of me to my
face, but I made a break with the things I used to
do and tried to stay around church-related things.

One of the first things God dealt with me
about was my sex life. As I began looking up different passages in the Bible on the subject of
purity, God revealed to me that my lifestyle was
wrong. I went to my boyfriend and told him we
could still see each other, but I wasn't going to
sleep with him anymore. He said okay at first,
but then he started harassing me, saying I was
crazy. I decided to be obedient to what God was
telling me, and it became a turning point in my
life. I broke up with my boyfriend. Even though I
experienced loneliness, God really blessed me for
doing what was right.

Before I became a Christian I went through
hell with guilt. Experiencing Christ's forgiveness
for my past has been one of the greatest healing
points of my life. It was like the burdens of my
past were just gone. Whenever I thought of something ugly from before, I said to God, "You mean
I'm forgiven for that too?" It was such a relief.

Then I met Jim, a dynamic Christian man. We
began a friendship and it was so pure. He always
listened to me and never judged me. Jim and I
sensed God's Spirit in our relationship. It wasn't
easy for me to stay pure, because I had placed a
lot of worth in my ability to please someone
sexually. But God took away that false sense of
worth and showed me that I am a special person
because I am in Christ.

Jim and I are now married and we have two
beautiful sons, Brandon and Eric. My past is forgiven and my life is changing more and more into
what Christ wants me to be. I still hurt inside
when I think of the two babies I aborted. I never
thought about what I was doing to them at the
time. I can't wait to see them in heaven. I want
them to know that I really love them and that
I'm sorry.

God has brought many people into our lives
who are thinking about divorce or abortion. Sharing with them from my experience is like pouring
an ointment on my inner wounds. Helping to
save a marriage or an unborn child helps continue the healing process in my own heart.

## PROCESS, NOT PERFECTION

As Susan's story demonstrates, God's power to heal
and change a broken life is alive and well, but her transformation didn't happen overnight. Coming to terms
with sexual regret and experiencing the freedom to love
again is a process, not an instantaneous occurrence. Our
hope is not in arriving at perfection in this life, but in participating in the process of God's power at work in us to
heal us and to change us day by day.

Furthermore, we don't always know what God's
process of change will include. We simply know that His
power will get the job done. I think about the story of evil
Manasseh, king of Judah. He was one of the worst kings
in Bible history, even going so far as to sacrifice his own
sons to pagan gods. In His anger, God allowed Manasseh
to be captured by his enemies, who put a hook in his nose
and shackles on his legs and dragged him to prison in a
distant country.

While in that dark prison cell Manasseh humbled
himself before the Lord and sought His favor, and a great

turnaround took place: "The Lord was moved by his entreaty and . . . brought him back to Jerusalem and to his kingdom" (2 Chronicles 33:13). God's power took Manasseh out of the dungeon and returned him to the throne. The process took many months, perhaps even years. But the Bible doesn't tell us how He did it or how long it took. It doesn't describe the steps along the way. We just see the results. We know it happened.

Similarly, our hope for healing and restoration does not rest in knowing *how* God will do it, but rather in knowing that God *will* do it in His own time and His own way. Our job is to keep ourselves actively involved in those things which will encourage the process of change in our lives. I personally believe the "Steps to Freedom" covered in Part II of this book are an excellent way to participate actively in the process.

Also, the process of growth and change is no guarantee that you will never fall again. Susan admitted to me that she battled with lust in her relationships with men for a long time after she became a Christian. The process of being perfected, not instant perfection, is the goal. If you fall along the way, confess your failure, pick yourself up again and get back in the process.

Perhaps the greatest requirement for your participation in the process is the determination to keep going. You will be tempted to ease up on the disciplines involved as you grow into your freedom. Don't give in to those temptations. Under Joshua's leadership the nation of Israel battled through Canaan claiming the land God had promised them. They got soft at the end, though, and didn't conquer every territory God commanded them to. As a result Israel was plagued by those undefeated enemies for centuries.

When I lived in Texas, my back yard was covered with weeds from fence to fence. I finally got tired of how bad the yard looked, so early one Saturday I got out the equipment and started assaulting the enemy.

By early evening I had cleared most of the yard of weeds. There were just a few tiny sprouts near the corners. I was tired and hot from my day's labor, so I decided to forget about the last few harmless little weeds. *They don't amount to anything,* I thought. *Besides, compared to what the yard looked like when I started, I can hardly see them.* I returned the tools to the garage with a great sense of accomplishment.

As you can guess, my pride in my back yard was short-lived. My schedule got hectic and I paid little attention to what was happening behind the house. During the next six months the few harmless little weeds I spared steadily sprawled from the corners to take over the whole yard again. The effectiveness of my one Saturday's hard labor had been nullified by my unwillingness to completely eliminate the enemy. I had gotten lazy and neglectful.

Don't make the same mistake as you begin marching through the process of healing from sexual regret. Decide now to submit to God's power in your life and cooperate with His process until you hear Him say, "Well done."

Before you can feel free to love again, it is important to understand the difficulties you face. In the next two chapters we will discuss the causes of the negative consequences of premarital and extramarital sexual activity.

# »»»» CHAPTER THREE ««««

## THE EMOTIONAL TUG OF WAR

Chris met Carl in a Dallas bar one summer while she was home from the university. Carl was the handsome man of her dreams. She fell madly in love with him and they dated steadily throughout the summer. He took her to expensive restaurants and trendy dance clubs. He prepared romantic dinners for her in his apartment and generously gave her money to spend on anything she pleased. Carl smothered Chris with attention.

Chris was so smitten by his advances that she couldn't resist his romantic invitations to bed. By the end of summer Chris was hopelessly hooked on Carl. She was also becoming disillusioned with his approach to romance. Sex with Carl was exciting at first, like forbidden fruit, but it wasn't everything that the movies and magazines made it out to be. Carl was aggressive and possessive.

Sometimes Chris felt he was forcing sex on her. Sex became increasingly distasteful to her and she felt a growing, subtle bitterness toward Carl within her heart. She secretly dreaded being alone with him, yet she desperately needed to belong to him.

Carl, a senior, and Chris attended universities in different states that fall. Though Chris dated other men, Carl was her major heartthrob. She wrote him long, romantic letters, and they spent several stolen weekends together during the school year. In their hotel hideaways, Chris got the closeness she wanted and, in exchange, gave Carl the sex he craved.

Finally Carl gave Chris his fraternity pin. Chris was ecstatic. Being pinned was one step away from being engaged. Her sorority sisters gave her the traditional candlelight ceremony in which she vowed not to date anyone but Carl.

At graduation, though, instead of proposing to Chris, Carl announced his plans to move to Washington, D.C., to work for a senator and attend law school — and he clearly did not invite Chris to come with him. Instead, he asked for his pin.

She was crushed. Carl had always talked about his thirst for power and his desire to become an influential politician. Chris suddenly realized that she had been little more to Carl than a pawn which he pushed around at will to gratify his quest for power over people. She had been used, abused and tossed aside.

After Carl left, Chris entered a period of severe depression which lasted more than two years. Her hurts and scars were deep. She thought she had been damaged beyond repair.

## THE UP SIDE OF SEXUAL INTIMACY

Chris is a good example of the emotional tug of war raging inside many individuals today which often ends up in sexual regret. Pulling from one side are all the reasons human beings seek sexual intimacy in the first place. This end of the rope reflects every good and positive attribute which God built into sex, all desirable, all to be enjoyed within a marriage relationship.

**First**, sexual involvement is desirable because *it makes us feel accepted and loved, even if only for a short moment.* "Someone cares for me." Sex often appears to be the doorway to a deep, meaningful, lasting closeness with someone. We assume that going to bed will automatically result in instant intimacy, and will fulfill our deepest desires for happiness.

Sexual intimacy does not *equal* love and acceptance, but, by God's design, it is *a major part* of meeting that need. Total, life-long commitment to a partner in marriage does not hinge on sex, but it does include it.

Sexual activity can lead two partners into a deeper emotional relationship, but for singles, the sense of intimacy will be superficial at best. Sex without marriage commitment will ultimately bring frustration and deeper loneliness. God's method by which singles are to meet their needs for love and acceptance is through developing close, caring friendships, loving God fervently, and getting significantly involved in other people's lives.

The **second** reason we desire sexual intimacy is that *it is exciting and fulfilling to a degree.* Our normal physical drives crave expression. Fulfilling these strong, natural drives through sexual intimacy is exhilarating.

God built those physical drives into us, and He has designed a framework in which to express them that will bring maximum benefits and lifelong fulfillment. The total intimacy we seek with another person, fueled by our inner drive for physical expression, can be experienced completely within the sanctity of the marriage commitment.

## THE DOWN SIDE OF SEXUAL INTIMACY

On the other end of the rope in this emotional tug of war over sexual intimacy are all the negative consequences of being sexually active outside God's boundary of marriage. This end of the rope can be summarized by the term *sexual regret*. It's the feeling of inner turmoil you have when you lose something you can never retrieve, or break something you can never repair, or commit a wrong you can never make right.

The inner pain and regret bring guilt, shame and remorse for violating God's directions concerning sex. Along with the regret comes the feeling that your personal happiness — or your potential for happiness — in a relationship is lost. The disappointment and disillusionment reflect the findings reported recently in a study of sexual activity in our culture: "There is a recognition that the emphasis on sex which typified the '60s and '70s has brought, not infinite human happiness, but some serious human misery."[1]

A young man approached me as I was packing up after a conference I conducted in his city. He wore the sad expression of someone who had just lost his best friend. He asked if I had some time to talk. I had to hurry to catch a plane, but I said we could talk while I packed.

"My girlfriend's best friend just told me that my girlfriend never wants to see me again," he began. "We've been dating for about five months and I thought everything was great. Can you tell me what went wrong?"

I had only a couple of minutes before leaving for the airport, so I asked him point blank, "Have you been going to bed with her?"

"Yes," he admitted. "She goes to bed with me and we love each other."

"There must be a miscommunication somewhere," I answered, "because she's left you. She may even hate you."

He reeled in surprise and shock, as if I had just slugged him. "She doesn't hate me. She loves me," he protested. "Why would she go to bed with me if she didn't love me?"

"If she really loved you, she wouldn't have walked out on you. If you took advantage of her emotionally and sexually, she's miserable inside. She resents you for violating her."

We talked for a few minutes more and then I had to leave. He never got the point. He didn't understand how his sexual aggressiveness could produce such negative inner turmoil for her. That's the negative emotional pull on the rope. Sex outside marriage has an emotional price tag: depression, guilt, disillusionment, haunting memories, fear, mistrust.

Negative emotional consequences from yielding to sexual pressures before marriage are often long-lasting. One man I know — I'll call him Barry — is on the brink of divorce from his second wife.

It all started during his first marriage when he was attracted to Tricia, a female co-worker in his office. At first they were just friends, but then they began spending more and more time together on coffee breaks and lunch hours. They shared jokes and stories with subtle sexual innuendos. They became increasingly familiar with each other physically, "innocently" hugging, patting and touching each other. Before long their smoldering passions burst into flame and they ended up in bed together and began a full-fledged affair.

Finally Barry divorced his wife and married Tricia. Then, after a few years at home with the children who came along, Tricia began feeling suspicious. She remembered that her relationship with Barry began in the office while his first wife was at home with *their* children. Now Tricia was at home and Barry was back in the office with other attractive, available women. Her suspicion grew into hostility and anger, and every time he came home fifteen minutes late she was convinced he had been fooling around.

Partners who are sexually active *before* marriage are often plagued by jealousy and anger for years *in* their marriage. They know from personal experience that their partners are capable of sexual intimacy *outside* marriage. The thought pattern goes, *If she was loose with me before we were married, she is capable of being loose with someone else now.*

Once I was the guest speaker on a radio talk show. After I had been interviewed, the host of the program opened up the phone lines and invited listeners to call in their questions to me. One woman came on the line sounding bitterly depressed.

"My husband is at work right now," she began, "and I have to talk to somebody. We've been married for eight years, but there's no love between us. He comes home drunk and physically abuses me. Our marriage started out to be wonderful; now it's a living hell. I don't know what happened to us."

I've heard similar stories before, so I voiced my suspicions in a probing question. "Were you and your husband involved in premarital sex?"

The woman paused. Then she answered, "Yes." She went on to tell that, before they were married, she and her husband not only abandoned their Christian values of sexual purity, but rebelled against their parents in choosing to marry each other. She agreed that possibly their rebellion against God and their parents had come back to haunt them in the form of mistrust, disrespect and abuse.

The long-term emotional cost of premarital and extramarital sex is like exorbitant, compound interest. You continue to pay, and pay, and pay—long after the enjoyment of your new purchase has worn off.

## CAUGHT IN THE MIDDLE

Unfortunately, in the emotional tug of war between the opposing poles of sexual purity and sexual promiscuity leading to regret, we are the rope. On one side we feel the steady pull of Bible-based moral standards urging us to postpone sexual intimacy until marriage.

On the other side we feel ourselves being reeled in—sometimes subtly, sometimes abruptly—by sexual temptations fueled by our drives, our old habits, our culture and the media. If we relax our moral standards in the slightest, we seem to be pulled even closer to compromise or to being dragged into the mud of sexual regret.

No one felt the tension more than Lynn. As a high school senior, Lynn was deeply involved in the full social scene—athletics, student government, parties and, of course, boyfriends. In Lynn's circles, boyfriends included sex, and Lynn was actively involved with her boyfriend.

During her senior year Lynn discovered the biblical message of Christ. She responded by trusting Him for forgiveness and new life. She changed drastically. The standard for her relationships and activities became the Bible and her faith in Christ. She got along better with her family and friends. Her weekend activities changed—and she broke up with her boyfriend.

"You mean you're not going to have sex again until you're married?" a friend asked her.

"That's right," Lynn answered confidently. And she meant it.

In the fall Lynn started her first year in college. She met a new group of friends, joined a weekly campus Bible study and found a Christian boyfriend. Rob was attractive, athletic and fun. He was as committed to leading a godly life as Lynn was. They enjoyed being together, and Lynn wished her former friends could see how she and Rob enjoyed a romantic relationship without sex.

But a month later the bottom fell out. She found herself lying in Rob's arms — in Rob's bed — sobbing with inner pain. *Is it possible, God?* she cried silently. *Is it possible for me to have a relationship with a man that will please You?*

Lynn had been pulled away from her convictions by passions she thought would never entrap her again. She was ashamed of her actions. She had gone back on her promises to God. She felt alone in her guilt with no one to talk to. Rob felt the same remorse for his actions, and they were no help to each other. They never discussed their painful feelings, and their silence about their guilt only drove them back to bed with each other. By January Lynn's pain and shame reached the depths as she became pregnant and then submitted to an abortion.

Lynn's emotional tug of war had stretched her to the breaking point.

## SHOW ME A WAY OUT

You probably know from experience what it feels like to be the rope in an emotional tug of war between purity and passion. Maybe you also know the pain of having your standards dragged through the mud in a moment of weakness, or maybe you're now in a relationship where your moral courage has been dissolved. Maybe you've been to the emotional depths like Lynn and Rob, or like Chris, the woman we talked about earlier.

Commitment to high moral values and a personal desire for sexual purity can be destroyed easily by moral rebellion and failure. Maybe you only slipped once, or maybe you are trapped in a habitual pattern of moral compromise. Maybe your experience of failure is in the past, but you are still chained to it by bad memories and mental anguish.

You may feel like a moral reject. You may feel worthless and hopeless, with nothing of value to offer God or a potential mate. You may assume that, since you have failed so often, restoration in God's sight (and your own) is an impossible dream.

So many people have asked me, "Is there anything I can do about my failure?" The answer is yes and no.

First the bad news: No, you can't go back through time and change the past. What's done is done. You may have to live with the consequences that your moral failure has brought into your life, but God can help you do that productively. In this sense, even the bad news has a positive side.

Now for the good news: Yes, you can rid yourself of poor choices and negative thinking so that your past experiences don't influence your present and future behavior. You need not be imprisoned by your past, no matter how discouraging it may be to you. You can come to terms with your sexual regret.

Yes, there is hope. For example, I wish you could see Chris and Lynn today. Both of them have been emotionally and mentally restored, and they have been released from the pain of their failures. Both of them are married to fine Christian men. Both of them are enjoying fulfill-

ing, godly families. And both of them are presently helping others who have suffered the consequences of sexual
immorality. If God can turn their lives around so
dramatically, He can do the same for you.

How did Chris and Lynn—and hundreds of men and
women like them I have counseled—get from the pits of
dismal failure to where they are today? How can you get
from where you are to where you want to be? I want to
show you the way by answering the following questions
you also may be asking:

- How could I have slipped into moral failure?
- How can God forgive me for what I did (or am doing)?
- How can I forgive myself?
- What can I do about the anger, discourage-ment and depression I feel about my failure?
- What can I do to rid myself of plaguing memories?
- How can I be useful to God again after what I've done?
- What can I do to prevent failing again?
- How do I get out of an immoral relationship?
- What is my hope for a future godly relation-ship with a person of the opposite sex?

Please keep in mind that no one will overcome the
emotional pain and scars of moral failure simply by reading a book. Change comes with action. Appropriating
biblically based principles and incorporating them into
your life will produce the change you desire.

Whatever happened to Barry, the fellow who married his former secretary? The last time I saw him was
in my office when I counseled him and Tricia, his second
wife. I'll never forget how hard-hearted he seemed. He

walked out of my office depressed. He didn't want to learn from his mistakes and submit his life to God. Instead he chose his own way. I heard he got divorced and now is with a third wife, repeating the same tragic pattern. He has never broken the cycle of moral failure and negative consequences. God calls that kind of person a fool (Proverbs 26:11,12).

Do you want to break the cycle? Then do it! You can learn and grow from your past. You can stop believing the lies about your being weak, and you can start living the truth about who God has created you to be. You can stop living with hurt, hatred and heartache and start living in Christ's power and love. You can win the emotional tug of war. You can be free to love again.

## »»»» CHAPTER FOUR «««««

## THE _____ MADE ME DO IT

One of the most popular television shows of the 1970s was a variety program starring comedian Flip Wilson. A highlight of each week's program was a hilarious skit featuring Geraldine, an irreverent, loose-living temptress, portrayed by Wilson dressed in gaudy women's clothes. Whenever Geraldine compromised her morals with her boyfriend Tiger or some other man, which apparently happened often, she had an excuse to free her from responsibility. Week after week, when confronted with her naughty behavior, Geraldine responded defensively in Flip Wilson's screechy, falsetto voice, "The devil made me do it."

Geraldine's laughable line became a tongue-in-cheek byword for irresponsible behavior, and the subtle idea behind it persisted in our culture long after Wilson's show left the air.

"The devil made me do it" seems to characterize our basic unwillingness to take responsibility for moral failures. We don't want to take the blame, so we look for the nearest likely scapegoat. If we don't blame the devil, we can quickly find something or someone else to take the rap.

When discussing premarital or extramarital sexual violations, who — or what — can we blame? If moral failure results in so much emotional turmoil, heartache and regret, why do we get involved?

Understanding the causes behind our sexual regret may help us come to terms with it better and be able to build a defense against a repeat of the problem.

Most Christians would probably agree that Geraldine's flippant reply, "The devil made me do it," contains at least a bit of truth. Moral purity is God's plan for men and women, and Satan is diametrically opposed to anything God has in mind for His people.

The apostle Peter wrote: "Your enemy the devil prowls around like a roaring lion looking for someone to devour" (1 Peter 5:8). Satan is responsible for tempting you to moral compromises and rejoices whenever you give in to them.

Yet in all the years I have counseled individuals and couples who came to me with sad stories of premarital or extramarital sex, not one person has said, "The devil made me do it."

No man has blamed Satan by saying, "He led me to drive her up to Inspiration Point at midnight and forced us into the back seat to go all the way."

Nor have I ever heard any woman say, "Satan led me to my boyfriend's apartment and enticed me to seduce him."

The devil can't *make* us do anything. Regarding the

prowling enemy, Peter admonishes, "Resist him" (1 Peter 5:9), and James promises, "Resist the devil, and he will flee from you" (James 4:7). Give Satan credit for his craftiness and persistence in temptation, but don't blame him for your willful act of moral rebellion.

Nobody I've talked to has filled in the blank in "The _____ made me do it" with "devil," but I've heard a lot of other excuses for sexual immorality which sound just as ludicrous. And that's what they are—excuses. I heard someone say that an excuse is the skin of a real reason stuffed with a lie.

## "IT'S HAPPENING ALL AROUND ME"

Some people claim, "My friends encouraged me to do it." I hear this a lot. They're referring to their peers, the crowd they run around with at work, in school, at the club, or in the neighborhood. They hear their friends talk about sexual exploits as matter-of-factly as if they had gone out to dinner or to a movie.

"All my friends are permissive in their sexuality these days," they tell me. "Getting intimate with your boyfriend or girlfriend is accepted in my crowd. Everybody does it."

This excuse draws its momentum from an even more widespread concept for escape from personal responsibility: "Society made me do it." Those who accuse society of contributing to their moral failure have a strong case.

As the Western World steps across the bridge into the 21st century, our moral standards continue to slide downward. The bed-hopping antics of the rich, famous and infamous, a subject once reserved for the sleazy checkstand tabloids, are now described in detail on the front page of the daily newspaper and on the nightly news broadcast. Movies which previously were confined to adult bookstores are now given an R or PG-13 rating for general viewing in "family" theatres and on television.

"No sex" has been replaced by "safe sex." Sexual abstinence before marriage is laughed at in our culture as prehistoric, Victorian or puritanical. Some sex education classes in public schools have gone beyond biological reproduction to teach students various techniques and methods for sexual intercourse. One class I heard about uses a video with plastic models of the male and female genitals to teach high school students the proper use of a condom.

Whether TV produces the decline in moral values or just reflects the sad situation, it affects millions of viewers. Think about it: Television was virtually unknown 40 years ago. But today's statistics show that 98 percent of all American homes have one TV and 55 percent have two or more.[1] The attitudes we see displayed on the TV screen demonstrate a disdain for sexual purity.

What are those attitudes? According to Ben Stein, author of *The View from Sunset Boulevard,* "The attitudes of the people who create television coincide with the picture on television."[2]

Robert Lichter and Stanley Roghtman interviewed 104 of the most influential executives, producers, directors and writers in the television industry to discover their attitudes on moral issues. According to the survey, 93 percent of them were raised in religious homes, but 45 percent claim no present religious affiliation and 93 percent seldom or never attend religious services. A majority take a permissive stance on the issue of sexual behavior, while only 17 percent strongly consider extramarital affairs to be wrong.[3]

Television has become a primary medium for displaying these values. Soap operas glamorizing illicit affairs now flood prime time as well as daytime TV. Dramas and sitcoms often subtly endorse convenient and indiscriminate promiscuity under the guise of love or just pure recreation. And the proliferation of satellite/cable TV and video cassette recorders has transformed millions of living rooms and hotel rooms into adult soft- and hard-porn theaters.

What are the results? Excuses. "If everyone else is doing it, why shouldn't I do it, too?" It's a convenient rationalization for their sexual misbehavior.

## "IT'S MY PARTNER'S FAULT"

Another excuse I often hear from people who become sexually involved outside of marriage is: "My boyfriend sweet-talked me into bed with him"; or, "My girlfriend pressured me"; or, "It was her sexy dress and flirty behavior that did it"; or, "If he hadn't stayed so long in my apartment after our date, we wouldn't have ended up in bed."

Men and women have been passing the buck like this ever since the Garden of Eden. When God pointed out Adam's disobedience, Adam put the blame on Eve, and Eve put the blame on the serpent.

Passing the buck is simply the fruit of self-centeredness. It is a cover-up, an attempt to escape the embarrassment of being found guilty of sowing wild seeds of illicit passion. For example, one partner says, "I love you so much. I just know that going to bed together will show our love for each other." At best, that statement is no better than a romantic hope-so; at worst, it's a manipulating lie. The person who gives in to that line will blame his partner later for his personal moral failure.

Or how about this one: "If you really love me, you'll go to bed with me"? Using this come-on puts a person's partner in an emotional hammerlock, and later that partner can excuse her behavior by saying, "He didn't believe I loved him. I was enticed to compromise my standards."

I've also often heard the following subtle deception: "It's okay for us to get involved sexually, because we're already married in God's sight." The person using this rationale is playing mind games. He is telling his partner that, since they're both committed to each other, and since they're planning to get married anyway, God will approve of what they do. The victim of this approach will likely blame the partner *and* God for his or her failure.

Whenever anyone tries to give me the married-in-God's-sight line as a valid reason, I say, "Show me the chapter and verse in the Bible that says two people can be married in God's sight without being married in a public ceremony." They can't do it, because there is no such verse. There also is no guarantee that their commitment will end in marriage.

## SELF-DELUSION

People who excuse their misbehavior as "my partner's fault" teeter on the brink of full-scale self-delusion in personal morality. They are the first to proclaim innocently, "We're not hurting anyone with our sexual involvement." Their blindness to the personal guilt, shame and heartache eventually will lead to an encounter with God for violating His plan for sex within marriage only. The problem is, they cannot see the potentially life-shattering consequences of their moral irresponsibility: devastating guilt, an unwanted pregnancy, a hasty wedding, an abortion or an adoption, lifelong disappointment, etc.

Another self-delusion statement I sometimes hear is, "After we get married we won't be tempted to yield to extramarital relationships like we did to each other." Someone who compromises his moral standards, and then thinks that marriage somehow will immunize him against further temptation, is living in a dream world. A wedding ceremony does not change an individual's character. If he yielded to temptation before being married, you can be sure he will be tempted do it again.

## "MY EMOTIONS RAN AWAY WITH ME"

Another flimsy excuse for premarital and extramarital sexual involvement is the claim, "My emotions made me do it." This individual argues, "We started getting romantic, and the romance soon turned into unbridled passion. Suddenly my urges took over and ran away with me, and I couldn't help myself."

This person is saying that at some point in the heat of a romantic encounter he became a romantic schizophrenic. His passion-fueled emotions suddenly became a separate entity and forced his mind and will to do something they really didn't want to do. "It wasn't my fault," he exclaims defensively. "I couldn't help it."

Similarly, some people blame their moral trouble on wanting to enjoy themselves. "We were just having fun," they insist, "and one fun activity led to another. One morning we woke up in bed with each other. We don't really know how it happened. We didn't mean any harm; we just wanted to have a good time."

My definition of fun is having a good time with no negative consequences. Going to a party is fun. Going to a party, getting drunk and waking up with a hangover is not fun. Going on a date is fun. Going on a date and waking up in bed with someone who's not your spouse is not fun, especially when the repercussions include guilt, frustration, etc. Everyone can come up with his or her own definition for fun, and that person must live with the consequences of that definition.

## "MY BACKGROUND WAS TOO STRICT"

Some people blame their parents for their moral missteps. They say things like, "My father wouldn't let me date until I was 16. Even then he demanded to know where I was going and insisted that I was home by ten. He was paranoid about my 'getting into trouble.' It's no wonder I rebelled and became sexually active. If Dad hadn't stifled me, I probably wouldn't have reacted so strongly against his morals."

Others claim the church was responsible for their rebellion against sexual purity: "The minister always preached against sex as if it were the unpardonable sin. In church I never heard anything good about sex, but my friends in school never said anything bad about it. I was tantalized by forbidden fruit and I had to try it for myself."

Rebellion against the rules of others brings a sense of excitement and power, but yielding to the temptation of premarital sex can backfire. Suddenly, after the marriage ceremony, the forbidden fruit is no longer forbidden. With the "legalization" of sex comes a diminishing of the adventure and excitement of daring to break the rules.

For individuals who were involved in premarital affairs, married sex can become boring and routine, often causing them to begin searching for forbidden fruit again —this time in extramarital liaisons.

## "NO PROBLEM — I'M FORGIVEN"

Perhaps the most insidious excuse for participating in sexual sin is to claim glibly, "It doesn't matter if I fall. God will forgive me anyway." The apostle Paul questions this individual with: "Shall we go on sinning so that grace may increase?" (Romans 6:1).

In other words, just because Christ has already forgiven all our sins, do we dare take advantage of His goodness and continue the very sins which sent Him to the cross?

Paul's answer is emphatic: "By no means! We died to sin; how can we live in it any longer?" (Romans 6:2). Forgiveness is not the issue; we already enjoy it. Cheapening God's grace is the issue. Continuing to commit sexual sin rejects God's call for personal purity.

God's desire for us is that we become like Him — holy (1 Peter 1:14-16). The result of living in sin is that we fail to experience His joy, peace and purpose.

## IT IS UP TO ME

At the beginning of the chapter I related a definition for an excuse: the skin of a real reason stuffed with a lie. As this thought-provoking definition suggests, all the excuses for moral failure I have mentioned in this chapter are coated with a veneer of truth. It's true that . . .

the pressure to conform to the lifestyle of sexually active friends, co-workers and an immoral society is great;

you can underestimate the influence of a romantically aggressive partner on your sexual behavior and responses, especially when the conditions of the date are inviting;

your sexual drives, your emotions and your passions can sneak up on you and surprise you with their power during a "harmless" romantic encounter;

the assurance of God's goodness and forgiveness can lull you into a false sense of security where you may find yourself repeatedly compromising God's standards of righteous living.

When you strip away the superficial veneer on these excuses, you expose the basic falsehood within them all: "I'm not responsible for my immoral actions; my circumstances are the cause of my downfall."

No one is a sexual zombie unwittingly victimized by the programming of circumstances. Obviously, I am not considering rape or child molestation at this point. Those are issues of an entirely different nature. We are dealing here with moral choices.

You are an individual with the ability to choose your own behavior. The first step in coming to terms with sexual regret is to take full responsibility for your moral choices, no matter how influential your circumstances may have been.

The most graphic example of moral failure in the Bible is the story of King David and Bathsheba as recorded in 2 Samuel 11 – 12. The story reads like the script of a modern soap opera.

As David surveyed the homes surrounding the palace from his rooftop one night, he spied beautiful Bathsheba bathing. After learning that she was the wife of Uriah, a leader in Israel's army who was away at war, David sent for Bathsheba and took her to bed.

When David discovered that Bathsheba was pregnant with his child, he initiated an elaborate cover-up for his misdeed which resulted in Uriah's murder. Then he married Bathsheba, who bore the son they had conceived illegitimately. Apparently David hoped his immorality was safely buried and that life in the palace would return to normal.

The Bible doesn't tell us what excuses, if any, David may have used to justify his adultery to himself. Perhaps he blamed Bathsheba for being so obviously visible to him from his rooftop. He may have thought that his passions got the best of him when Bathsheba arrived at the palace. Maybe he felt his behavior was an excusable reaction against the commandment strictly prohibiting adultery. Whatever his reasoning, though, God wasn't about to let David off the hook so easily.

The Lord sent the prophet Nathan to confront David with his sin. To his credit, David didn't try to worm his way out of responsibility by billowing a smoke screen of lame excuses. He owned up to his adultery: "I have sinned against the Lord" (2 Samuel 12:13).

David realized that he was responsible to God for what he had done. It was not enough to admit his offense to Nathan and to change the course of his behavior. To be sure, he had violated Bathsheba, murdered Uriah and lied to the entire nation by covering up his sin, but in his formal confession David pinpoints the crux of his failure: "Against you, you only, have I sinned and done what is evil in your sight" (Psalm 51:4).

Moral failure is a choice against God. Personal responsibility for sin must begin with accountability to the Lord Himself.

There is bad news and there is good news concerning David's sin and his later transparency of personal responsibility. The bad news concerns the negative consequences David experienced, even after he confessed to Nathan and to God. For one thing, the son David and Bathsheba had conceived out of wedlock lived only seven days after birth. For another thing, as Nathan predicted in 2 Samuel 12:10-19, David himself was the victim of family strife and warfare for years. Moral failure often brings with it painful consequences, and they don't necessarily go away just because you own up to what you have done.

The good news is that David's sin didn't disqualify him from being used and blessed by God. Despite the problems in his life after his adultery, David is still known in Scripture as a man after God's heart (Acts 13:22). David was a model worship leader and the composer of many of the greatest hymns ever written, the psalms. In Psalm 78:70-72, one which David did not write, he is hailed as a man of integrity in his leadership of Israel.

There's good news for you too. As you face up to your moral failure and take full responsibility for your participation in it, God will help you move forward to experience all that He wants to do in you and through you.

## »»»» CHAPTER FIVE ««««

## ON THE ROAD TO RESTORATION

If anybody needed to be restored from the ravages of sexual regret, it was Rick. His story is best told in his own colorful, honest words:

Most people's first impression of me goes something like this: intelligent, gifted, better-than-average looks, personable, normal. Some say I'm mysterious to the point of being threatening. Others find me deep to the point of being different. I guess you can't please everybody, but most people tell me that God gave me a fair share of the goodies in life.

Whatever the reasons are, I've always seemed to be attractive to women, and I've dated a bunch of them. Lookers. Thinkers. Devout. Devoid. Locker-room-story women. Women with empty heads and full bras. Women with deep minds and shallow cups.

Then, once upon a time, I met a beauty named
Anna. She was immensely friendly. Easy to
know. Positive. These pluses were countered by
her blatant immaturity and questionable character and substance, but I must honestly confess, I
was too busy staring at her boobs to see her heart.

I must admit I've not always been the Prince
Charming type to the loves of my life. Anna happened to enter my life at the right time, though. I
was 28, tired of first-date questions, tired of the
dating ritual, tired of being single. From the start
I did my best to be my best with Anna. My old
girlfriends would have been amazed to see the
patience, sensitivity and commitment I invested
in her. (Anna needed all those qualities — in
abundance.)

As we approached our second anniversary of
dating, I was making secret plans to propose to
my fair maiden, while she was making secret
plans to dump me. She caught me completely by
surprise — which hurt. Part of the surprise was
finding her sharing the sheets one weekend with
an old boyfriend — which hurt even more.
Another part of the surprise was staring into
eyes that just days before burned red hot with "I
love you," and finding those same thick-lashed
eyes filled with Texas-Chain-Saw-Massacre indif-
ference — which hurt the most.

Two years. Cuddling. Talking. Fighting and
making up. Evolving from pretentious early
dates to comfortable, couch-potato Friday nights.
All the stuff said, all the stuff understood. Two
years of building hacked and maimed in just a
day. The relationship was buried in a closed-
casket funeral.

Afterward, I sat alone with little smithereens

of my heart bleeding on the carpet. It had been an emotional amputation without anesthetic. Put a stick in your mouth and bite down hard as she started sawing.

Enter God. Or, more accurately, re-enter God. I had held His hand a long time ago, but somewhere in the growing up stuff I let go of God and moved on to women, and to Anna.

I am a preacher's kid, born with a spiritual silver spoon in my mouth. Although other kids had more money, more stuff, cooler vacations, etc., I had the greatest gift: two walking-talking, second-by-second Christian parents. I experienced a personal relationship with God very early. God was not abstract to me; He was real. I knew more about the Bible than fifteen seminary students. Even as a boy I had moved on from David and Goliath stories to the foundational principles of the Bible, principles like "you reap what you sow."

The reaping after Anna was awful. I remember sitting at my desk, numb, inhaling and exhaling thick, sharp pain even Tylenol III couldn't dull. I've broken my leg and my nose before. Give me that kind of pain any day. Just don't break my heart. The fragile Waterford crystal decanter where my soul had lived had been crushed and my soul sloshed around through the broken glass. I felt alive only on some warped basis of the philosopher Descartes's statement: I hurt, therefore I am. My cells hurt. My atoms hurt. My DNA hurt.

As I sat with my feet propped up on my desk and my heart down somewhere between the chair and the floor, I knew I had to pray. I debated it. Who was I to ask Holy God for help? How hypocritical! How cheap! My intellect said no. It took nearly an hour to quit the debate.

The first words were the hardest.

"Dear God . . . "

I had no idea what to say next, but I knew at my deepest, deepest level that praying was *exactly* the right thing to do. I knew without a doubt that He, my Creator, was literally listening to me. It was just little me and big Him. Only utter honesty would do. I was scared to go on, but mortified not to. "I'm embarrassed to pray to You. I have absolutely no right on earth to pray to You."

At that moment, for the first time in my life I saw myself accurately. More important, I saw God accurately. I couldn't pray this prayer on the basis of brownie points, good deeds done, favors accumulated. His absolute holiness and my absolute dirtiness were as real as my inner pain. This gap between His glory and my tragedy wasn't some temporary thing, the result of my separation from Anna. I realized that, even in my happiest moments with Anna, I had been so miserably distant from His wonder that life seemed utterly hopeless.

I couldn't go one word further in my prayer until I grasped this reality. God was letting me see a sliver of truth—and the truth fit.

Then I laid out my whole story to Him. It was undoubtedly the most sincere prayer I'd ever prayed. There was no pretense, no formality. I doubt if many of the words I muttered contained more than one syllable.

I told God that I was upside down, inside out. I was honest with Him about my predicament, about my pain and about taking responsibility for

what I had done. My confession wasn't circum-
stantial or related only to Anna issues – I stood
before God like Adam without even one fig leaf of
rationalization to cover myself.

There came a point in my prayer when I felt it
was God's turn. It seemed He was either going to
fry me with a lightning bolt or totally ignore me.
I would have preferred to be fried. I couldn't face
the thought that God had written me off.

I may have been sitting in my chair, but my
soul was prostrate on the floor, waiting. God's
response wasn't a spoken message in my ear or a
handwritten message on the wall. It's like that
old question, "If a tree falls in the forest when no
one is around, does it make any sound?" If you're
within hearing distance, you'll hear it. God's
answer to my prayer was like a tree falling inside
me. No telling how many trees have fallen in my
inner forest. This time, for the first time in my
life, I was within hearing distance.

What did I hear? Forgiveness, love. I suddenly
knew that this great, pure, holy God loved me
and forgave me. I wasn't hoping for forgiveness; I
knew I was forgiven – then and there, for everything. I felt vacuumed, freshly painted, spring
cleaned.

Up to that point, love, forgiveness, grace,
peace and faith were nothing more than nouns in
my religious dictionary. Astonishingly, one by
one, the rote Sunday school definitions of these
terms were replaced by the reality behind the
definitions. I was no longer just an eyewitness to
love and forgiveness; I was a participant.

My encounter with God that day was only the
beginning. The pain didn't evaporate, which was
good because the pain kept me on my knees. I

never let go of God's hand. I'd wake up in the
morning, make a long-distance call to Him and
never hang up. We stayed on the line together all
day. The healing was phenomenal. In October I
was Lazarus in the tomb: dead and gone, a stink-
ing mess.

By mid-January I had "come forth."

## NEW LIVES FOR OLD

Rick's story illustrates the wonderful things which
can happen when a morally stained, damaged life falls
into the hands of the Master Restorer.

I love antiques, especially antique oak furniture. I
love to take an old desk, table or chair, and painstaking-
ly strip off the layers of paint or varnish and refinish the
wood. I gain great personal satisfaction in restoring the
original luster and glory to a piece of furniture which has
been dulled by time and neglect.

I wonder if God experienced a similar sense of satisfaction as He lovingly and patiently worked in Rick's life
to bring him back him from the hurtful, damaging effects
of sexual sin and regret?

Before we meet Christ, we are like so many pieces
of junk furniture locked away and forgotten in a dusty
warehouse. Our original beauty and luster are dulled
through disobedience and rebellion, but God sees our in-
herent value underneath the layers of sin. When we place
our faith and confidence in Him, He brings us out of the
back room of the dusty warehouse store and rescues us
from the dominion of darkness and brings us into the
kingdom of the Son He loves (Colossians 1:13).

In effect, salvation moves us into the workshop of
the Master Restorer of human lives. The change of own-
ership is instantaneous—from death to life, and from

darkness to light. Yet, much like the restoration of antique furniture, stripping away the vestiges of the old life and restoring the beauty of the original creation is a time-consuming process. Little by little, step by step, the layers of the past are cleansed away and the God-given beauty increasingly shines through.

You may fear that your immoral lifestyle has permanently stained and damaged your life, but the Master Restorer is ready to go to work, just as He did in Rick's life. As you submit to His craftsmanship by setting out on the road to restoration, He will strip away the blemishes sin has caused and restore the original beauty of what He created you to be.

Perhaps you have tried to change your illicit activity time and again, only to fall prey again — each time. You feel discouraged and defeated by your continued failure. You've confessed your sin many times, but deep inside you wonder if God has already given up on you. Maybe you've been a Christian for a long time. You thought you were immune to sexual temptation, but you succumbed and now you're crushed and embarrassed by your fall. You may be thinking that your life can never be the same again, but the Master Restorer is ready and able to cleanse away the crud of sexual regret and return the God-given beauty to your life.

The road to restoration actually begins with a decision based on Galatians 5:19-25. You really have only two choices in life, and those choices parallel the two lists in these verses. On one hand, you can choose to ignore God's instructions concerning moral purity and give in to "the acts of the sinful nature . . . : sexual immorality, impurity and debauchery; idolatry and witchcraft; hatred, discord, jealousy, fits of rage, selfish ambition, dissensions, factions and envy; drunkenness, orgies, and the like" (vv. 19-21). But if you choose to dabble in this behavior, you're not choosing the road to restoration, but the sad road to further pain and bondage.

On the other hand, the road to restoration begins with a choice for life in the Spirit. The apostle Paul describes the kind of restorative work God seeks to produce in us through His Spirit: "The fruit of the Spirit is love, joy, peace, patience, kindness, goodness, faithfulness, gentleness and self-control" (vv. 22,23). In fact, committing yourself to pursue life in the Spirit through Christ is the only way to purge yourself of the presence and power of the sinful passions and desires which formerly scarred your life (vv. 24,25).

If you're ready to choose the fruit of the Spirit for your life instead of the fruit of the flesh, the rest of this book is for you. It will show you step by step how to follow God's principles to experience the forgiveness and restoration you seek.

## THE CLEAR PICTURE

Setting out on the road to restoration requires that you establish your alliance with God and declare your allegiance to Him afresh as Rick did. This is a critical step because your moral failure is a direct result of substituting another god for God in your life. That's right: As illustrated by Israel in the Old Testament, acts of immorality are the result of involvement in idolatry. It seems Israel was always being drawn away from the Lord to serve the gods of the heathen nations around them. Whenever they embraced the first "I" sin—idolatry, the second "I" sin—immorality—was not far behind.

The root of your moral problem is pride. The attitude is "I'll do it my way." You have set yourself, or someone of the opposite sex, or your passions, on the throne which God is to occupy in your life. When God is evicted from the throne of authority in your life, His standards for morality are usually thrown out with Him, and moral failure is the result. We lack the power to obey and be victorious.

Idolatry was Israel's most frequent temptation and greatest failure. God apparently knew how great the problem would be, because the first two of the Ten Commandments deals with the topic of idolatry (Exodus 20:3-6). Other subjects were covered adequately with only one commandment each, but idolatry was so serious that it alone received the double-barreled treatment.

The many negative consequences of premarital and extramarital sex are tragic enough, but the greatest consequence is the loss of intimacy with God Himself. His clear purpose for His people is for them to behave in a manner that pleases Him, to live a holy life. In fact, the New Testament word for a Christian is *saint,* which means "holy one."

Many people look at the idea of a holy life as one of boredom. "You want to be pure? Don't you want to have any fun?" What they don't realize is that the greatest adventure is living in close relationship with God. And talk about fun? God offers it *along with* satisfaction, peace of mind *and* purpose in life.

Nevertheless, there is a catch. We have to live God's way. He did not ask us for advice when He set up the rules, and He is not asking us now.

There are a lot of good reasons to avoid immorality. The best reason is that God says it is wrong. It doesn't matter what anyone else says about it, the clear statement in the Ten Commandments is: "You shall not commit adultery" (Exodus 20:14).

Jesus took it a step further by showing that adultery is more than the behavior of two people sharing sexual intimacies outside marriage. Adultery involves thoughts in a person's mind: "You have heard that it was said, 'Do not commit adultery.' But I tell you that anyone who looks at a woman lustfully has already committed adultery with her in his heart" (Matthew 5:27,28).

Then the apostle Paul put the final nail in the coffin of fuzzy thinking with: "It is God's will that you should be holy; that you should avoid sexual immorality" (1 Thessalonians 4:3).

The road to restoration is not just a process of changing your behavior or standard of morality by correcting old habits and activities, although some changes will need to take place. Restoration must begin by returning Christ to His rightful place as Lord of your life. You can't live a Christ-honoring, moral life without Christ and His moral values at the center of your life.

That's what makes this book so different from the many self-help, current psychology books on the subject of relationships. Changing your moral behavior is not primarily the result of a formula of sure-fire steps for success. True, there are some practical things you can and should do to come to terms with your problem, and later in this book these Steps to Freedom are explained in detail. The transformation in your life, though, must spring from a change of alliance, a whole-hearted recommitment of your life to Jesus Christ. Without the foundation of God and His standards at the center of your life, any results gained will be short-lived.

Furthermore, in and of yourself you don't have the power to heal the hurt or repair the damage your failure has done to your mind, emotions and passions. As Rick discovered, only God can do that. Without His presence at the center of your life, not only are you destined to repeat your immoral behavior, but you also are destined to remain mired in the pain and negative memories.

You need the power of God residing within you to heal your sexual regrets from the past and change your behavior in the future.

## CHAPTER SIX

## THE WAY OF RESTORATION

As you prepare to embark on the seven "Steps to Freedom," there are some things about the restorative process you should keep in mind. These are the signposts along the way which will help you stay on the right road and keep you moving forward.

### THE SIGNPOSTS

1. *Get back to the Bible.* Be aware that restoration from sexual regret implies a return to biblical values. Along with your renewed allegiance to Jesus Christ must come a firm commitment to God's moral code as found in the Bible. That means that the attitudes and activities which God labels wrong and prohibits in Scripture, you must also label wrong and exclude from your behavior.

No matter how society, your peers, your boyfriend or girlfriend, or your sexual urges may object, God's Word is your standard. You will not experience God's restoration in your life if you don't decisively embrace His standards for your morality.

2. *Beware of pitfalls.* Restoration does not mean perfection. Following the Steps to Freedom is no guarantee that you will never again be tempted to moral failure or that you will never fall to those temptations. In fact, once you re-align yourself with God and His values concerning sex, you may find yourself experiencing even greater temptation.

Unfortunately, Rick became a painful example of this principle. As the miraculous restoration from his sad affair with Anna progressed, Rick knew that he needed to go on what he termed a "girl-free diet" for several months. He was going to play it straight, slow and Christian in his future relationships. Then he met Callie, whom he described as "a committed Christian, a living checklist of the qualities any sensible guy would desire in a wife."

Their relationship moved extremely fast, "a Johnson-Space-Center kind of liftoff," Rick remembers. The restraints Rick had promised himself burned away in the heat of his whirlwind romance with Callie. His commitment to sexual purity also fell by the wayside again. The relationship crashed almost as quickly as it had taken off. Rick, now in the process of restoration again, is more gun-shy than ever about trusting himself in a relationship with a woman.

Taking a stand for moral integrity is kind of like announcing that you are going on a diet. When your friends hear about your plan to lose weight, they seem to go out of their way to dangle fattening desserts in front of you. Why? They may want to have a good laugh, or they may feel guilty about their own weight problems. If they can keep you from reaching your goals, it will make them feel better by comparison.

Similarly, when you tell your girlfriend or boyfriend that you will no longer hop into bed with them after a date, they may become more aggressive about being physically intimate with you. No one likes to be rejected, and sometimes the reaction is to be even more possessive.

In addition, expect spiritual battle, because the devil will attack your movement toward God and His righteousness. Rely on the power of the Lord to defeat the enemy's schemes. "The one who is in you is greater than the one who is in the world" (1 John 4:4).

Be alert that the road to restoration contains many pitfalls. Your commitment to travel the road does not assure uninterrupted success, but the forgiveness and power of God are always available as you pick yourself up and keep going.

3. *Take it nice and easy.* Restoration is usually a slow, steady process, not an instantaneous achievement. True, some attitudes and activities can change overnight. Trust God to bring quick changes as you take definite actions to follow His ways. In many ways, however, this is a lifetime journey, not just a snap-of-the-finger transformation. Traveling the adventurous road to restoration means steadfastly focusing on the long haul. You can be sure that, as you keep moving forward, you *are* changing, even though some changes may be barely perceptible to you. Your daily motto should reflect the feelings of the man who said, "I ain't what I ought ter be . . . and I ain't what I'm gonna be . . . but, thank God, I ain't what I used ter be, nither!"

There are plenty of examples of long-term transformation in Scripture. For forty years in the Midian desert God developed Moses into the mighty leader of the na-

tion of Israel. Christ worked with Peter for three years
to mold him into one of the chief pillars of the first-cen-
tury church. It took many years after the Damascus Road
encounter for Christ to build Paul into a dynamic leader.
From a Roman prison, Paul spoke of the transformation
which continued in his life:

> Not that I have already . . . been made perfect, but I press
> on to take hold of that for which Christ Jesus took hold of me.
> . . . I press on toward the goal to win the prize for which God
> has called me heavenward in Christ Jesus (Philippians 3:12,
> 14).

Let me encourage you — restoration can be steady
and sure. Press on toward the dynamic thought life and
lifestyle God has designed for you.

4. *Take that first step.* Every journey, no matter
how long, begins with the first step. Standing on the
threshold of the process, you may feel intimidated because you don't know much about God or the Bible. Perhaps you're a brand new Christian. Or maybe the pain
of your moral failure has freshly opened up a long-dor-
mant relationship with Christ. Or maybe you feel unsure
that you can live up to God's moral standards after failing so badly in the past. For one reason or another, you
feel ill-equipped for the journey and hesitant to start.

You don't need to meet some lofty standard before
you can set out on the road to restoration. God knows exactly where you are, and He accepts you at that point. He
is aware that your feelings of inadequacy make your
failure look like a mountain to you, but He invites you to
step forward and begin to grow. You don't need much to
get started — only a little faith in a great God. You have
His assurance that . . .

> if you have faith as small as a mustard seed, you can say to
> this mountain, "Move from here to there," and it will move.
> Nothing will be impossible for you (Matthew 17:20).

5. *Don't travel alone.* Progress on the road to res-

toration is achieved by an unbeatable combination — you and God. As you faithfully align yourself with Christ, He brings significant development and growth. It's your responsibility to take all the positive, practical steps you can to deal with your sexual regrets, but you can't change yourself, your past, your present or your future. Only God can do that. Be confident that, as you apply yourself to moving ahead obediently, God will respond by performing His restoration in you as only He can. "Come near to God and he will come near to you" (James 4:8).

## TIPS FOR YOUR STEPS TO FREEDOM

As you prepare to venture out on the road to restoration, consider the following tips. They will help make your journey more meaningful and profitable:

1. *Find a quiet place to study.* The Steps to Freedom should be thoroughly examined and carefully studied. Reading through them only casually will greatly minimize your potential for change. In order to realize the greatest benefit from the following chapters, you need to find a quiet place where you can delve into them without interruption. Also select a time of day when you will have the highest level of privacy and concentration for your study and for prayerful application.

2. *Keep your Bible handy.* The Steps to Freedom are based on scriptural principles. As you study each step, look up the Scripture references in your Bible and read them for yourself. Then in the margins of this book, or in a notebook, jot down the insights you gain from Scripture which apply to your life and relationships.

3. *Move through the steps at your own speed.* Study Step 1 and Step 2 thoroughly and focus on appropriating God's forgiveness and on forgiving yourself. Then scan the remaining five steps and select the next one you want to study based on which one you feel you need next. For

example, you may presently be battling the temptation of impure thoughts in your mind. Perhaps you should move to Step 4. Then you may want to jump ahead to Step 6, fall back to 3, move on to 5, return to Step 4, etc. Design your order of study to meet your unique needs. You may even want to memorize the titles of the steps in order to know clearly the road to restoration.

4. *Continue studying as you grow.* Since growth in the area of moral integrity is a continuing process, your study of the Steps to Freedom also should be continuous. Reread the seven steps often and apply new insights to your life. Try reading a different step each day of the week in order to let these principles soak into your heart and mind. Study other relevant biblical passages so you will know thoroughly all that God says about the topic.

5. *Find a partner to share with.* Ask someone to hold you accountable for what you are learning on the road to restoration. Ask your boyfriend or girlfriend to study the Steps to Freedom also, and talk and pray with that person about what you are learning. Or maybe you can find a trusted friend of the same sex who will become your study and prayer partner. If you can't find someone who is willing to study the book with you, at least ask someone (a friend, a parent, a pastor, a Sunday school teacher, etc.) to pray for you and allow you to share with him or her what God is doing in your life as you work through these steps.

6. *Look at the "Quotes by God."* Beginning on page 161, this section is a series of biblical passages on topics we will discuss. When you have questions or face temptations, read those relevant verses. Even better, memorize them. If your friends have misconceptions about what the Bible says about sexuality and purity, share with them what God says. The more you understand His actual quotes, the more you will live by His exciting principles. You can't go wrong by following His directions.

»» **PART II** ««

---

STEPS TO FREEDOM

# »»»» STEP 1 «««««

## ACCEPT GOD'S FORGIVENESS

Experiencing God's forgiveness is the first and most basic of all the steps to freedom from sexual regret. Apart from His forgiving work in our lives, there is no hope. You can try to clean up your act and turn your life around — and you may even succeed to a certain extent. However, without God's forgiveness you have dealt only with surface issues and not the heart of the matter. If you don't deal with your sin and guilt before God, all your efforts to change will ultimately fail, because your problem is first and foremost a spiritual problem.

As King David revealed in his confession, moral impurity is a sin against God even more than it is a sin against another person (2 Samuel 12:13; Psalm 51:4). Since the first level of offense is against God, the first level of restoration must be forgiveness from God.

In your failure, you may have wronged another person, such as the boyfriend or girlfriend with whom you shared sexual intimacy, and you may need to apologize to that person and ask for his or her forgiveness. Important as that step may be, though, it is secondary to the step of seeking and accepting forgiveness from the primary one you have offended — God.

Another reason for seeking and accepting God's forgiveness as your first step is that you are guaranteed immediate and complete success. God will never hold a grudge against a truly repentant person, nor will He stand off at a distance until you have suffered awhile under the weight of your guilt. When you confess your sin, He forgives and forgets your sin at that moment. The slate is immediately and completely clean. It's the one step to freedom you don't need to repeat. Once it's done, it's done. You can move on with your life confident that the primary offense — your sin against God — has been dealt with and washed away. Subsequent steps to freedom may require persistent discipline on your part, and success in them may come slowly or in stages, but you can enjoy God's complete forgiveness right now.

## "IF WE CONFESS OUR SINS"

The basis for accepting God's forgiveness is the familiar Christian's "bar of soap," 1 John 1:9: "If we confess our sins, he is faithful and just and will forgive us our sins and purify us from all unrighteousness." Let's look at this verse piece by piece in order to understand and apply its truth to our experience of moral failure.

In order to receive God's forgiveness, we must recognize and admit our impurity for what it is: sin. In the Old Testament, the Hebrew word for sin literally means "to miss the mark," as an arrow which misses the bull's eye on an archery target. The word emphasizes man's total inability to hit the bull's eye of God's demand that we be like Him — righteous and perfect. The New Testament word for sin means to turn aside from God's expressed will. Our pride chooses to go wrong constantly. We have a fallen nature that is disobedient to God and rebels against his laws. "All have sinned and fall short of the glory of God" (Romans 3:23).

Perfection is also God's standard for moral purity. Paul wrote to the Ephesian church: "Among you there must not be even a hint of sexual immorality, or of any kind of impurity" (Ephesians 5:3). To the Corinthian Christians he wrote: "Flee from sexual immorality. All other sins a man commits are outside his body, but he who sins sexually sins against his own body" (1 Corinthians 6:18).

There it is in black and white: sexual immorality — even a hint of it — is sin. You may say, "But I'm not a loose-living, immoral degenerate. I just blew it once in a moment of weakness." It doesn't matter to God. Missing the mark by an inch is as good as missing it by a mile. Sin is sin, and it must be confessed for what it is in order to be forgiven.

First John 1:9 directs us to confess *our* sins. We are personally responsible for what we have done. Admittedly, there are many pressures which bombard us daily, influencing us to abandon our moral values. The source of sin is our pride which wants to do things our way.

If you watch sexually oriented movies, absorb the suggestive lyrics of today's popular music, fantasize with lurid novels, or listen intently as your friends describe their sexual exploits in detail, you will be involved in mental immorality. *Lust is a normal desire gone wild.* It changes the beauty of God-ordained married sex into self-gratifying conquest of another person. You make that choice yourself; nobody makes it for you. You are responsible for your behavior.

In *Beyond Choice,* Don Baker cites a counseling situation between a pastor and a young woman named Debbie who had three abortions. Debbie complained to the pastor that, because her parents required her to have her first abortion, they were responsible for all her moral problems.

The pastor strongly refuted Debbie's claim. He did agree that Debbie's parents may have contributed to some of her problems, as had society in general, her boyfriends and other circumstances of her life. Nevertheless, he challenged Debbie to accept full and complete responsibility for all that had happened to her: "Your problems did not begin with your abortion. They began in your mind when you first started developing your relationship with Tim Beezley [Debbie's first boyfriend]. When you refused to say no to Tim in the back seat of that car, for whatever reason, that was when your problems finally passed beyond your ability to control them."[1]

In order to experience God's forgiveness, you must admit your responsibility for your sin. Other people and circumstances may have influenced your behavior, but ultimately the choice was yours. To confess sin means simply to agree with God's perspective of your behavior and humbly admit to Him, "I'm wrong and You're right."

That's what David was doing when he wrote:

> Against you, you only, have I sinned and done what is evil in your sight, so that you are proved right when you speak and justified when you judge (Psalm 51:4).

Confession sweeps away all the excuses and openly states to God, "I did it."

## FORGIVENESS FOR **SIN** AND **SINS**

You are not first guilty before God because you have committed immoral acts, but because you are basically self-centered and rebellious. You have a sinful nature that affects your attitudes and actions, and that puts you in the position of being cut off from God. Apart from God's forgiveness, you are doomed to be . . .

> punished with everlasting destruction and shut out from the presence of the Lord and from the majesty of his power on the day he comes to be glorified in his holy people and to be marveled at among all those who have believed (2 Thessalonians 1:9,10).

The good news is that Jesus Christ carried your sin and guilt to the cross and they died with Him there (1 Peter 2:24). The penalty of eternal separation from God has already been paid and your sin has been forgiven (Colossians 2:13,14). The Bible says, "When this priest [Jesus] had offered for all time one sacrifice for sins, he sat down at the right hand of God" (Hebrews 10:12). Why did Jesus sit down? Because the work of forgiveness was complete. Some people say that forgiveness means the slate has been wiped clean. I believe the Bible confirms that the slate has not only been wiped clean — it has also been thrown away. His message is total forgiveness.

When you come to understand the truth and reality that Christ's death on the cross and resurrection were for you, the way is open for you to enjoy an intimate, eternal relationship with God. His forgiveness cleanses you from all sin — your sin nature as well as specific sins you have committed — and saves you from the horror of condemnation and from eternal separation from Him. The only thing left for you to do is accept the gracious provision God has already made for your forgiveness. Believing God to do what He says He will do is called faith.

Have you personally entered a relationship with Jesus Christ by accepting forgiveness for your sin and committing your life to Him? If you have not, would you like to establish a relationship of oneness with God? It is yours if you put your faith in Him. His promise is, "Whoever hears my word and believes him who sent me has eternal life and will not be condemned; he has crossed over from death to life" (John 5:24).

If you long for this special love relationship with your Creator, I invite you to put your faith in Christ. Take a moment right now to pray and open your heart to Him. Confess your need for Him to cleanse you and give you a new life. He will come into your life and set up His residence there for all eternity (Revelation 3:20). You may want to pray a prayer similar to this:

*"Lord Jesus, I need You. Thank You for dying on the cross for me. Enter my life and forgive my sins. I know You have answered my prayer and have totally purified me."*

## "HE . . . WILL FORGIVE US OUR SINS"

Once we admit our sin to God, His forgiveness is immediate. At that instant God separates us from our sin and its penalty. The separation is complete, final and eternal — the sins God forgives are gone forever.

A beautiful picture of what happens at forgiveness is found in Psalm 103:12: "As far as the east is from the west, so far has he removed our transgressions from us."

I'm intrigued by the fact that the psalmist described our separation from sin as east from west instead of north from south. If you start at the North Pole to journey around the world, you will only travel south until you reach the middle of Antartica. As soon as you pass the South Pole, you will be traveling north until you return to the North Pole, at which point you will start south again.

On the other hand, if you circle the earth by traveling eastward along the equator, you will always travel east. There is no point on the globe where you will stop traveling east and start traveling west, unless you make a 180-degree turn and begin traveling in the opposite direction. Once you start heading east you continue in an easterly direction to infinity.

Had the psalmist declared that our sins are removed from us as far as the north is from the south, we could measure the distance — approximately 12,500 miles from pole to pole. Instead, he stated that our sins are removed from us as far as east is from west — an immeasurable distance. It's impossible for us to tell where east ends and west begins. I think God was trying to show us that His forgiveness is so thorough that neither we nor He will be able to find our sins again. What a wonderful, liberating picture!

Some people with whom I share this truth about God's great forgiveness get a mischievous gleam in their eyes. "When I commit a sexual sin and then confess my sin," they probe, "does God forgive and forget that sin forever?"

"Yes," I assure them, "God's Word says that."

"And if I commit that sin again, and then confess it again, God will forgive me again?" they pursue.

"God's grace is without limit," I answer.

"Then I can go on enjoying sex, and as long as I keep confessing my sins, God will keep forgiving me and I will be okay, right?" they conclude.

My answer is, "Right *and* wrong." God's infinite grace, His unmerited favor toward sinners, is certainly broad enough to cover all your sins — past, present and future — without limit.

However, as I stated earlier, although such an arrangement is possible, the apostle Paul challenged that attitude with: "Shall we go on sinning so that grace may increase? By no means! We died to sin; how can we live in it any longer?" (Romans 6:1,2). That's called "cheap grace," wrongly presuming upon God's forgiveness.

God generously grants us forgiveness, but He also calls us to a change of behavior. At the same time that Jesus refused to condemn the woman caught in adultery, He also challenged her, "Go now and leave your life of sin" (John 8:11).

Furthermore, continuing to sin and then repeatedly claiming God's forgiveness will result in some serious personal problems. I like to illustrate this point with a block of wood, a handful of nails and a hammer. You can pound nail after nail into the wood, then pull them out and throw them away. Obviously, after the nails are gone, the holes in the wood will remain, and the more nails you drive into the wood and pull out, the more scarred the wood becomes.

Your sexual sins, like the nails, can be removed and thrown away by confession and forgiveness, but each sin leaves an ugly scar, a nail hole, in your life. Physical, mental, emotional and spiritual consequences will conflict with the quality of moral purity God wants to build into your life. Also, each disobedient act, even though it is forgiven, contributes to the building of a habit pattern of negative behavior. The more often you commit an act, the more difficult it is to break that pattern.

Though God's grace is great enough to cover a lifetime of sins, we must respectfully receive His forgiveness and seek to rid our lives of those sinful patterns of behavior. When we realize that His kindness has saved us from destruction and torment, our hearts respond with thanksgiving and a deepening desire to live a holy life.

The critical question is: Do you love Him? Jesus said,

> If you love me, you will obey what I command . . . Whoever has my commands and obeys them, he is the one who loves me. He who loves me will be loved by my Father, and I too will love him and show myself to him (John 14:15,21).

If a person truly places his faith and trust in Jesus Christ and what He did for him on the cross, the Holy Spirit dwells inside that person. He, the Holy Spirit, is grieved when we sin (Ephesians 4:30). It's pretty hard to imagine a person recklessly going about sinning knowingly and then expecting God to forgive and forget. This person really doesn't love Christ, nor does he have a clear picture of what God's love, grace and forgiveness are all about.

## "AND PURIFY US FROM ALL UNRIGHTEOUSNESS"

Not only did repentant David confess his sin to God, but he also asked God to cleanse him of his sin and renew his purity:

> Cleanse me with hyssop, and I will be clean; wash me, and I will be whiter than snow . . . Create in me a pure heart, O God, and renew a steadfast spirit within me. Do not cast me from your presence or take your Holy Spirit from me. Restore to me the joy of your salvation and grant me a willing spirit, to sustain me (Psalm 51:7,10-12).

Many people who attend my conferences and hear me talk about God's forgiveness for sexual sin have a hard time believing God can cleanse them. They turn in messages on their response cards which read: "It's too late for me to be forgiven"; "I've been too bad for too long"; "I believe God can forgive me for other sins, but I don't think He can forgive me for going to bed with my girlfriend."

For some reason, many people think moral sins are worse than other sins. They feel that God isn't as willing to forgive moral failure as He is to forgive "lesser" sins like cheating on an exam, gossiping or bursting out with angry words.

The Bible gives no indication that sexual sins are any worse than other sins. However, even if they were, 1

John 1:9 promises that God will purify us from *all* unrighteousness. The only qualification is faith. Whatever sins we confess, believing in God's promises, He forgives — no exemptions, no exclusions. Moral sins may have more social implications than other violations of God's law, but they are as forgivable and "cleansable" as any personal failure.

No matter how badly you may have fouled up your life morally, the Lord Himself guarantees that your life can be cleaned up. Your regret must lead to repentance and confession — changing your mind about your sin and agreeing with God that it is wrong. Repentance means to desire for God to change you, to make every effort to turn from past godlessness and choose obedience and purity. You need to develop a new pattern for thinking by letting God renew your mind (Romans 12:2; Colossians 3:2). Your thought patterns should lead to new patterns of behavior. As Josh McDowell points out:

> Ask God what fruits of repentance you need to show. It might be breaking off a relationship. It might be making major lifestyle changes. It might be not frequenting certain types of places again or not watching certain kinds of movies or TV programs. It also might be limiting your dates to double-dating situations. It could be any one of a number of other things, anything you know is wrong for you.[2]

We will talk more in later chapters about lifestyle changes necessary for traveling the road to restoration.

## THE FRUITS OF BEING FORGIVEN

The example of David's confession resulting in His being cleansed illustrates two attitudes that accompany accepting God's forgiveness. The **first** is an attitude of *joy*. Life brings no greater exhilaration than that of knowing that the sin which separated you from God has been cast away forever. David exulted: "My tongue will sing of your righteousness. O Lord, open my lips, and my mouth will declare your praise" (Psalm 51:14,15). Forgiveness of sin is reason enough to praise God for eternity.

Les Carter, in *Mind Over Emotions,* echoed David's outlook:

> The guilty person will readily admit that he truly deserves the wrath of God, but when he realizes God's desire and willingness to forgive no matter how great the sin, there is a feeling of unrestrained gladness. There is a warm inner comfort and security that results from being loved and forgiven by God the Creator.[3]

The **second** attitude which accompanies forgiveness is *humility.* After David admitted his sin, opened himself to God's cleansing and received His forgiveness with praise, he was a more humble man. He wrote:

> You do not delight in sacrifice, or I would bring it; you do not take pleasure in burnt offerings. The sacrifices of God are a broken spirit; a broken and contrite heart, O God, you will not despise (Psalm 51:16,17).

The prophet Micah also recognized the importance of humility in an individual's relationship with God: "What does the LORD require of you? To act justly and to love mercy and to walk humbly with your God" (Micah 6:8).

When you realize you are harboring immoral actions or lustful thoughts, you don't need to drown yourself in regret or self-condemnation, but you should experience a genuine, humble sadness. This will accompany the process of confessing sin and accepting God's forgiveness. Paul wrote: "Godly sorrow brings repentance that leads to salvation and leaves no regret" (2 Corinthians 7:10).

Although this emotion may be painful, it is beneficial in order for you to change and to ward off similar temptations in the future.

Do you believe God still loves you despite the immoral choices in your past? Believe it—He does! Do you believe God can forgive you completely for what you have done? Believe it—He can and He will! As you conclude this chapter, put down the book and spend some time talking with God. Ask Him to shine His holy light into your heart. Make a list of your sins, the ones the Lord brings to your mind. Confess them in detail to Him. Admit to Him that you are wrong and He is right about what you have thought and done. Write 1 John 1:9 across the entire list, and then destroy the list. Remember: The message of the cross of Christ is total forgiveness. Your sins are gone and forgotten. Believe Him. He never lies.

Then praise the Lord for forgiving and forgetting your sin and for placing infinity between you and your specific sins. The issue is now settled forever. You may continue to thank God for your forgiveness, but you never again need to ask God for forgiveness of those specific sins.

You are now ready to move on to Step 2.

>>>> **STEP 2** <<<<

## FORGIVE YOURSELF

The conference was over and a number of people had gathered around me with questions and comments. As I visited with one person after another, I noticed a young woman lingering at the outer edge of the group. She had a look of concern on her face, and she acted nervous and flighty. She obviously wanted to talk to me, but was waiting until all the other conference attendees had left.

This happens a lot when I speak about sexual purity. Among those who attend are always a few who have a heartbreaking load of guilt and who are searching for answers. They are usually so embarrassed about their problems that they are last in line waiting to speak with me. When the crowd has gone and I face these individuals one-to-one, I know each one is ready to drop a bombshell on me.

This woman was no exception. When we were finally alone she introduced herself and thanked me for my contribution to the conference. Then she got to the point.

"I've known Christ for several years," she began with a slight quiver in her voice. Small tears spilled from the corners of her eyes. "I'm a respected leader in the Christian organization that sponsored this conference. But I got involved with a man some months ago, and now I have VD. Nobody knows except my doctor . . . and you."

In my efforts to comfort and encourage her, I talked to her about the importance of confessing her failure to God and accepting His forgiveness. She assured me that she had done so, yet obviously something else troubled her deeply. So I kept probing with questions. Finally after several minutes she tearfully blurted out her deepest pain. "I know God has forgiven me, but after what I've done I don't deserve a decent man. And I can't bear the thought of living the rest of my life alone."

This woman's story illustrates the inner struggle of countless numbers of people who have violated their sexual purity. They have relied on the grace of God, they have confessed their sins, and they have received His forgiveness—but they can't let themselves off the hook so easily. They understand God's ability and willingness to forgive them, but they seem neither able nor willing to forgive themselves.

## A DIFFICULT SECOND STEP

This second step to freedom from sexual regret is often more difficult to take than the first. For some reason we have little problem with God's part in granting forgiveness. First John 1:9 is so deeply ingrained in our hearts that we believe beyond all shadow of doubt that He is capable of forgiving us. He is sovereign and He is omnipotent.

We're also all too aware that *we* are *not* sovereign or omnipotent, so we say, "I'm glad God has forgiven me, but I can't forgive myself."

There are several reasons you may be unwilling to forgive yourself for sexual sin. **First**, *you may feel you still need to be punished* for what you have done. You know your moral failure was a violation of God's law, and, even though you have accepted His forgiveness, you still feel guilty. Or you feel duty-bound to "pay." The woman mentioned earlier was denying herself the possibility of ever marrying a "decent man."

Punishing yourself is a futile attempt to clear your conscience. If you want to earn your standing with God, you must be absolutely perfect — and your sexual sin has already proved you're not. The punishment for even the slightest deviation from God's standard of perfection is death — complete separation from God. It's a case of all or nothing. No other punishment will do the job.

Now, if you are a Christian, God already has accepted you eternally and He won't let you go. There's no way you can pay any part of the price for your sin. You need to realize that the entire penalty has already been paid. Christ's death on the cross, in your place, covered all your sins — past, present and future. There is nothing you can add to His provision, so why not stop trying, and forgive yourself? Simply accept His gift.

A **second** reason you may have difficulty forgiving yourself is that *you don't feel you deserve forgiveness.* You may be thinking, *I wasn't tricked into moral compromise. I walked into it with my eyes wide open. I knew I was opening myself up for trouble when I invited him to my apartment for a cozy dinner for two. I recognized the point at which our romantic evening started becoming more passionate than we had planned. I knew exactly where we were headed, but I did nothing to stop it. I sinned with* *full knowledge of what I was doing. I can't forgive myself for that.*

The solution to this argument is that 1 John 1:9 makes no distinction between intentional and unintentional sins. As discussed in chapter 4, you are ultimately responsible for what you do. Whether you meant to fall into your sexual sin or not makes no difference. God has promised to respond to your confession of sin by purifying you from *all* unrighteousness.

Yes, you must deal with your tendency to put yourself in compromising positions. That's what the remaining five steps will help you do. In the meantime, you must accept the fact that sin is sin and that God has forgiven you from all of it. On that basis you deserve to forgive yourself.

**Third**, you may not be ready to forgive yourself for your sexual sin because *you're convinced you will repeat it*. "I know I'm weak in this area," you complain, "and I'll probably fall in the future. How can I forgive myself for something I know I'll do again and again?"

Beware: This argument for not forgiving yourself is often an excuse to continue in sin. It's true that Christians aren't perfect. As one church's liturgy suggests, we sin in thought, word and deed every day. That's no reason, though, to yield to sin and ignore God's gift of forgiveness. God's grace and power is available every day too. Jeremiah the prophet states:

> Because of the LORD's great love we are not consumed, for his compassions never fail. They are new every morning; great is your faithfulness (Lamentations 3:22,23).

Your response to God's great compassion and faithfulness should be to confess each day's sins to Him. Then accept His forgiveness and forgive yourself for your failure. Determine daily to walk in obedience and purity, and ask God for the strength to do so. When you slip, don't wallow in your sin just because you fell again—take advantage of God's grace. Confess again, immediately pick yourself up again and allow yourself to keep growing toward maturity.

## FORGIVE AS GOD FORGIVES

If you have experienced God's forgiveness, but fail to forgive yourself, you are telling God that His forgiveness is not enough. Think about it. By not forgiving yourself you are saying, "Nice try, God, but You don't realize how bad I am. You have forgiven me, but that's not enough to cover my sin." It's a pretty serious charge to accuse God of not knowing what He's doing. In effect, that's what you do when you refuse to confirm His forgiveness by forgiving yourself.

When you forgive yourself, you simply participate in and affirm what God has already done. God's activity concerning our sin is beautifully summarized in the New Testament book of Hebrews, which quotes from the Old Testament prophecy of Jeremiah:

> "Their sins and lawless acts I will remember no more." And where these have been forgiven, there is no longer any sacrifice for sin (Hebrews 10:17,18).

At the moment you confess your sin to God, two wonderful things happen simultaneously: He forgives it and He forgets it. When we human beings talk about forgetting something, we refer to a lapse of memory. For example, your roommate asks you to buy a half-gallon of milk on your way home from work. When you walk through the door that night empty-handed and your roommate says, "Where's the milk?" you say, "Oh no, I forgot!" Somewhere in your brain the message to bring milk home got lost.

Almighty God is not like that. He doesn't suffer from any lapses of memory. Nothing inadvertently slips His mind. God can only forget something on purpose, not by accident.

That's what He has done with your confessed sin. He has consciously and purposefully willed to forgive it and forget it — and anything God wills to do gets done. So your sin is completely and eternally blotted from His memory. "I, even I, am he who blots out your transgressions, for my own sake, and remembers your sins no more" (Isaiah 43:25).

The Old Testament gives several picturesque descriptions which help us understand why it is impossible for God to remember what He has forgiven and forgotten.

Job claimed: "My offenses will be sealed up in a bag; you will cover over my sin" (Job 14:17).

Isaiah wrote: "You have put all my sins behind your back" (Isaiah 38:17).

What a mystery. The God who sees everything has purposely placed your sins in a place where He can no longer see them.

The Lord also said through Isaiah, "I have swept away your offenses like a cloud, your sins like the morning mist" (Isaiah 44:22). Just as the fog is burned away by the morning sun, your sins have utterly evaporated in the warmth of God's love and forgiveness, never to be seen again. Micah closed his prophetic message with these words of encouragement: "You [God] will tread our sins underfoot and hurl all our iniquities into the depths of the sea" (Micah 7:19).

Consider the vast, completed work of God's forgetfulness! It challenges us with beautiful freedom: "Blessed are they whose transgressions are forgiven, whose sins are covered. Blessed is the man whose sin the Lord will never count against him" (Romans 4:7,8). In other words, God has forgiven and purposely forgotten your confessed sins forever. You are truly blessed. When you do not validate God's forgiveness by forgiving yourself, you live a defeated life as if your sins were *not* forgiven. It is imperative for your spiritual health and growth that you forgive yourself for the sexual sins you have confessed to God.

## EASIER SAID THAN DONE

The theology of God's forgiveness is clear in Scripture, and the importance of affirming God's forgiveness by forgiving ourselves is certainly implied in Scripture. Now, how do we do that? Where is the bridge which leads from the fruitless pall of personal unforgiveness to the freedom of walking out from under that cloud? The key to walking in the freedom of forgiveness is more in what you *know* than in what you *do*. When you get a firm grasp on the following two basic truths about yourself as a Christian, you will find your problems with self-forgiveness will begin to disappear.

### 1. Know that you are accepted "in Christ."

No phrase in Scripture defines who you are as a Christian more completely or concisely than the two words "in Christ." Paul used "in Christ" 133 times in his letters. The phrase means that, as a believer in the Lord Jesus Christ, you are always intimately one with Him. There is nothing about you which is outside of Christ. Since you have accepted Christ by faith, He has completely accepted you.

You may be wondering, *How can someone like me, who has a history of moral impurity and still suffers temptation to moral failure, be accepted in Christ?* Through total forgiveness, which is the very nature of being in Christ.

Paul wrote: "In him we have redemption through

his blood, the forgiveness of sins" (Ephesians 1:7). If you weren't forgiven, you couldn't be in Christ. The resounding message of the New Testament, especially Paul's writings, is that your faith in Christ has solved your sin problem once and for all and you are accepted in the beloved.

Study the book of Ephesians carefully and write down all the wonderful things that are true of you because you are in Christ. The more you are infected by Christ's unconditional love, the easier it will be for you to accept and forgive yourself.

## 2. Know that you are being transformed by the Holy Spirit.

Paul paints a vivid contrast between the individual controlled by sin and immorality and the individual who is in Christ:

> Do not be deceived: Neither the sexually immoral nor idolaters nor adulterers nor male prostitutes nor homosexual offenders nor thieves nor the greedy nor drunkards nor slanderers nor swindlers will inherit the kingdom of God. And that is what some of you were. But you were washed, you were sanctified, you were justified in the name of the Lord Jesus Christ and by the Spirit of our God (1 Corinthians 6:9-11).

Your history as a sinner may not be as sordid as Paul's description, but before you met Christ you were dead in your sin, devoid of any spiritual life. When you placed your faith in Christ at salvation, not only were you placed into Christ, but Christ, through the working of the Holy Spirit, was placed into you. He came in to give you spiritual life and to transform you inwardly.

Being placed into Christ was instantaneous and complete. You can't ever be in Christ any more than you were at the moment of salvation. That's why He completely accepts you.

On the other hand, the transforming work of Christ in you through the Holy Spirit is a lifelong process. As you follow Christ day by day, week by week, month by month and year by year, you are being changed inside (2 Corinthians 3:18). Your old sinful habits are giving way to new patterns of righteous behavior. Your old thoughts are being replaced by thoughts of purity.

One of Satan's greatest ploys is to trick you into living in the past instead of growing into the future. If he can keep you discouraged and dejected about your failures in the past — both before and since becoming a Christian — he can impede the transformation process the Holy Spirit is affecting in you. For example, as you think about the sexual sins you have committed and confessed, Satan can drag you into the defeating "if onlys": "If only my parents had been stricter with me about sexual purity"; "If only I had read the Bible and prayed more instead of spending so much time fantasizing about my boyfriend"; "If only we hadn't gone to Inspiration Point alone"; "If only I hadn't filled my mind with so many erotic novels, movies and magazines"; etc.

You can't change or relive your past, so why try? Your past is history. It is beyond the transforming activity of the Holy Spirit. Use the memories of it as lessons to help you grow today and tomorrow. Allow your failures to reveal weak spots you need to shore up with prayer and perhaps professional counseling. Use your unpleasant memories of places you got into trouble as warning signs to keep you away from those places in the future. Let your bad experiences with certain people coach you about the kind of people you shouldn't hang out with.

And, of course, be thankful for time. Time has a way of erasing the bad memories as you *choose* not to dwell on them. Your memory is similar to a river. As more water runs into the river from its tributaries it becomes deeper and wider. So it is with our thoughts and memories. The more you mull over in your mind the details of what happened in the past, the deeper those events are ingrained in your memory. You must cut off that river of memory by choosing not to think about those events, and create a new river by thinking about positive events.

Whenever you feel guilty about moral failures you have already confessed to God, use that feeling as a springboard to praise the Lord. Instead of cowering under false condemnation, begin to thank God confidently that these sins are forever forgiven and forgotten. Get alone and praise God aloud for forgiveness. Or meet with a trusted Christian friend and ask him or her to join you in putting guilt to flight through praise and thanksgiving.

Satan not only uses our past to trip us up, but he also uses the temptations of the present to stunt our spiritual growth. Whenever you feel lonely, or are being tempted toward immoral thoughts or deeds, spend some time applying your identity in Christ. Say aloud, "I am in Christ and I am completely accepted by God. I am a changed person through Christ's transforming work in me by the Holy Spirit." You will soon find yourself agreeing with God wholeheartedly that you are forgiven and free.

## »»» STEP 3 «««

## EXPECT POWERFUL CHANGES

A few years ago I was captivated by a front-page story in a Dallas newspaper. It told about a man who attended an exhibition where beautiful rocks and gems were on display. The man walked up and down the rows of displays until he came to a small box of rocks on a table. A sign advertised that the rocks in the box were $15 apiece. The man rummaged through the box until his eyes fell upon one particular rock. "I'll give you ten dollars for this one," he said to the man behind the table.

"Well, business has been a little slow today," the proprietor replied. "Sure, you can have it for ten bucks."

The man paid for the rock, then walked outside the building and gave a shriek of joy.

He was a gemologist — an expert in precious gems. The rock he had purchased for ten dollars was a star sapphire, the largest star sapphire ever discovered in America, worth two and a half million dollars!

I've often wondered how the proprietor felt when he read the story in the newspaper. He didn't realize what great value was hiding in his box of rocks. He was a millionaire and didn't even know it! He must have been shocked and heartbroken when he learned that the rock he had sold for ten dollars was worth a fortune.

## A VALUABLE POSSESSION

A lot of Christians are like that man with the box of rocks. We have the most valuable possession in all the world, something that no amount of money can buy: the wealth of God at our complete disposal. Yet we often live like spiritual paupers, like people who have nothing. We see our weaknesses, our failures and our sins, and we say, "I'll never be what God wants me to be. I don't have what it takes to live a life of moral integrity. I'll never change."

Wrong! You are a spiritual millionaire; you just don't know it yet! Your life can change for the better because you have God's riches at your disposal. The secret to success is learning how to get God's wealth into your walk. You can successfully march through the Steps to Freedom when you realize that God has already equipped you with everything you need to do so.

To understand what God has done for us and provided for us, look at these incredible words from the pen of the apostle Paul: "Praise be to the God and Father of our Lord Jesus Christ, who has blessed us . . . with every spiritual blessing in Christ" (Ephesians 1:3). Paul does not say that God *will* bless us, or that He *is* blessing us now, but that He *has* blessed us. It's past tense; it's already happened. God has already blessed you with every spiritual blessing and resource for a successful, pure life.

You may be thinking, *Wait a minute, Dick. I don't feel blessed. I have problems. I stumble around. I do the wrong things. And I have trouble doing the things God wants me to do. Maybe I was absent the day God passed out these blessings.*

The key to understanding our spiritual blessings is in the prepositional phrase "in Christ." That's where our spiritual blessings reside. They are reserved for us in heaven in the person of Jesus Christ. If we are in Christ, and God's blessings are in Christ, we are in touch with God's blessings for us, because it's all inside the same relationship.

You must understand that everything I'm talking about here is directed to people who are in Christ, those who have committed their lives to Jesus Christ, who have personally put their faith in His death and resurrection. If you are not in Jesus Christ, the wealth of His spiritual blessings is not accessible to you. You need to be in Him to receive His blessings.

The secret of the successful Christian life of purity and integrity is wrapped up in one word: faith. Faith appropriates God's blessings in Christ, which are already reserved for you and waiting for you, and brings them into your daily walk. God's wealth already belongs to you. If you want to know how wealthy you are in Him, read Ephesians 1:4-14. All these blessings became yours the moment you received Jesus Christ, regardless of how you feel. You just need to reach out and take them.

## A VITAL LINK

The link between possessing God's wealth and appropriating it by faith into your daily walk is found in Paul's prayer for the Ephesian Christians: "I keep asking that the God of our Lord Jesus Christ, the glorious

Father, may give you the Spirit of wisdom and revelation, so that you may know him better" (Ephesians 1:17).

Notice the two things Paul prayed for. **First**, Paul wanted the Ephesians to have a *spirit of revelation*. That means he wanted their minds opened to things they have never seen before.

What did Paul want the Ephesians to see? That which would help them "know him better." The Greek word *know* means "full knowledge." Paul was literally praying, "Lord, fill their minds with everything a human being can know about You." Wow! Couldn't you live victoriously if you knew all you could know about God? That's what God's revelation can do.

**Second**, Paul prayed that God would give the Ephesians a *spirit of wisdom*. Wisdom is what we need to help us live out what we know about God. Full knowledge of God is useless without the wisdom to know how to act on what we know. It's like those cartoon caricatures showing people with huge heads and tiny bodies. God doesn't want us out of proportion like that, our heads filled with knowledge while our actions are small and insignificant. Getting God's wealth into your walk is a balanced combination of revelation and wisdom, growing in your knowledge of God and in your godly actions.

## SPECIFIC ACTIONS

In addition, Paul wrote:

> I pray also that the eyes of your heart may be enlightened in order that you may know the hope to which he has called you, the riches of his glorious inheritance in the saints (Ephesians 1:18).

Paul continues his prayer by pinpointing three specific measures you can take to transfer God's wealth into your personal walk. As you make these three positive moves, you will experience power for permanent change in your life.

**Action 1. Settle Your Future** ("know the hope to which he has called you")

Paul is not using the word *hope* like we often use it. We say, "I'm planning to play tennis, so I hope it doesn't rain"; or "I hope it snows so I can go skiing"; or "I hope our team wins the championship." That kind of hope is merely wishful thinking.

The kind of hope Paul prayed for each believer to have is the settled assurance that something you have yet to see is going to happen. For example, we read the words: "In all things God works for the good of those who love him, who have been called according to his purpose" (Romans 8:28). Notice, the verse doesn't say all things are good. It says that all things *work* for your good. That verse requires hope. You may not be able to see any good in a death of a loved one, but hope can see beyond the tragedy to the good which God will bring out of it. Also, there is nothing good in an act of sexual impurity which fills you with regret, but the hope to which God calls you sees beyond your failure to the good which He has promised to bring out of it after you have turned it over to Him.

Notice also that this verse doesn't apply to everyone in the world. It only applies to those who love God. God will take all the events and experiences that have taken place in your life and work them out for your good. Even if your past includes sexual sin, God can work it out for good in your life if you truly love Him and seek to do His will.

You can exercise hope even in bad situations because God has a purpose for you. Notice the next verse: "For those God foreknew he also predestined to be conformed to the likeness of his Son, that he might be the firstborn among many brothers" (Romans 8:29).

What is God's purpose for those who love Him, those

He foreknew? To mold them into the image of Jesus Christ, to produce Christ's character in them—and He aims to keep up the process until it is completed (Philippians 1:6).

John the apostle wrote:

> Dear friends, now we are children of God, and what we will be has not yet been made known. But we know that when he appears, we shall be like him, for we shall see him as he is (1 John 3:2).

When Jesus Christ comes back, and we all go up to meet Him in the air, you'll look at Jesus, then you'll look over at your friends and say, "My goodness! They have characteristics just like Jesus Christ!" They'll look at you and say the same thing. That's God's purpose for us and that's why we can continue to have hope even in the darkest circumstances.

Let me illustrate hope another way. A friend of yours recommends you see a certain movie. "It's an unbelievable thriller," he says. "All I will tell you is that the hero gets the girl."

So you go to see the movie. It's tense and exciting. The bad guy is shooting at the good guy, and the good guy gets hit. There's blood everywhere and it looks like it's over for the good guy, but you're relaxed because you know the end of the story. Your friend said that the hero gets the girl, so you know the good guy is going to live.

Then a bunch of the bad guys kidnap the girl and threaten to blow up a city if they don't get the ransom money. The fuse on the dynamite is burning down and the girl is squirming to wriggle out of her bonds. Everybody in the theater is on the edge of their chairs—except you. You know how it turns out, so you just sit there waiting to see how she's going to get away.

Your life is a lot like that movie. You go through problems, disappointments and tough times, and you experience temptations and regrets. People tell you one thing and do just the opposite. You get confused in the pressure and turmoil—but you know the end of the story. God is working out His purpose by reproducing the image of Jesus Christ in you. That kind of hope can help you settle your future.

No wonder Paul could write from a Roman prison: "Rejoice in the Lord always. I will say it again: Rejoice!" (Philippians 4:4).

We are tempted to say, "Paul, are you crazy? You're in prison. If something doesn't happen soon, you're going to die there."

Paul replies, "You don't understand. Prison is not the issue. God's purpose in me is the issue. God is at work through my circumstances to make me like Christ."

That's the settled, confident hope you need to face the future. No matter what confronts you, God is making you like Jesus. He is fulfilling His purpose in you. You can either help Him in the process or drag your feet by questioning your circumstances and doubting that He can get you through them.

When I was single I had a problem trusting God for the future. I wanted to get married, but I didn't have any prospects for marriage. I also knew that, when I found someone I liked, I should wait six months to a year before getting engaged. Then I figured I'd be engaged at least six months before getting married. Occasionally, I would get very discouraged. *It's not fair,* I thought. *I'm getting older by the minute and I'm still at least a year and a half to two years away from getting married. I don't even have a woman I'm interested in.*

Then I began to think about Christ. He knew what I was going through. He died at age 33 as a single man, but His life was anything but a failure. I experienced tremendous joy in the middle of my struggle as I realized

I wasn't alone. God had my future under His control. He had a purpose for my life which far exceeded my temporal concern about marriage. I determined to cooperate with God's purpose of making me like Christ. I would walk in faith and let God do what He wanted in my life to produce the character of Christ in me. I was ready to take on anything, because my future was settled. I knew the end of the story.

**Action 2.  Value Your Worth** (know "the riches of his glorious inheritance in the saints")

We know from Paul's letter to the Christians at Rome that we have inherited eternal life, heaven, and many other blessings from God by becoming co-heirs with Christ through faith. This second part of Paul's prayer in Ephesians 1:18 isn't talking about *our* inheritance; it's talking about *God's* inheritance.

What is God's inheritance? It's "in the saints." I used to think a saint was a big stone figure of some deeply religious person who lived back in the Middle Ages. According to the Bible, every Christian, past and present, is a saint, meaning "holy one." Paul addressed most of his letters to the churches as he did to the Ephesians: "To the saints in Ephesus" (Ephesians 1:1). If you have received Jesus Christ personally, you are a saint.

So what is God's inheritance? You and me! Before we were in Jesus Christ, we were lost. God was our Creator, but He was not yet our Father because we were slaves to sin. Because of the death and resurrection of Jesus Christ, and our faith in Him, we became the children of God (John 1:12; Romans 8:15,16). Thanks to the life and work of Christ, God has inherited everyone who comes to Him through faith in Christ. Don't you feel special knowing that you are God's inheritance?

I was seven years old when I opened my life to Jesus Christ. I often have imagined what the scene in heaven must have been that day. Here is an angel romping around the golden streets in purity and perfection, having a great day as usual. Suddenly he looks down and sees this seven-year-old kid folding his hands, bowing his head and asking Christ to come into his life. The angel turns to another angel and says, "Oh, no. Look who's coming into God's family now. It's that little Purnell kid. It's going to be a job keeping him on the straight and narrow path. This means double overtime for all of us."

The angel in my imagination was right. During the years following my decision, I struggled as a growing Christian. I was always doing the wrong thing at the wrong time for the wrong reasons. I was a hypocrite much of the time. I'd promise God, "I'm going to live for You, God," and I'd do it — for about 15 minutes.

When I get to heaven I only want to ask God one question: "Why did you ever put up with me?"

God will simply reply, "Because you're My child, My pride and joy, My inheritance."

It's beyond my understanding, but I'm certainly glad God feels that way about me.

If you are in Christ, you are of great value to God. You are His inheritance, His treasure. You have some great prospects for change and growth in your life because you are extremely valuable to God and God takes care of what belongs to Him. He is even more interested in your development as a person of integrity and purity than you are. What's more, He has what it takes to mold you into the person He wants you to become.

## OUR PROBLEMS WITH SELF-ESTEEM

If we are so valuable to God, why do we have so many problems with self-acceptance and self-esteem? I think there are three reasons.

**First**, *we have a misconception of God.* We think God is a big ogre in the sky who is against fun and happiness. We picture Him hovering over us with a baseball bat. As soon as we smile or start having fun, *wham!* — He hits us with something bad. "I knew it," we say. "God's out to get me."

We feel God doesn't like us very much and that He's just waiting to punish us, but that's not the scriptural picture of God at all.

**Second**, *we have problems with our self-worth because we compare ourselves with others.* We say, "Lord, look at this wimpy body of mine. I wish I looked like that person with the good-looking body." We wish we had another person's talents and abilities, personality, or a hundred other things that we envy.

What we're really saying is, "God, You need a little counseling. You missed the boat when You made me. Let me tell You where You went wrong."

God didn't make a mistake when He made you. You are so absolutely special to God that, when He made you, He threw away the mold. There's no one in the world like you; never has been, never will be. Don't compare yourself with anyone else, because you are incomparable. That's how privileged you are as God's unique creation.

**Third**, *we struggle with our self-worth because of our past sins.* You got yourself into trouble through sexual impurity. You asked God to forgive you, and He did. Yet every time you try to do something for God, or think about studying your Bible, or think about talking to somebody about Jesus Christ, past failures flood your mind.

"Remember what you did two years ago?" your feelings taunt you. "You've even repeated it several times since. You'll never amount to anything."

We end up believing the lies of Satan and relegating ourselves to being second-class Christians.

When you feel put down because of your past sins, remember that God's royal blood is flowing through your veins. Jesus Christ spilled His blood to forgive your sins and present you to the Father as His inheritance. Yes, we must walk in humility before Him because we don't deserve His grace. At the same time, though, we can walk also in confidence and strength because God values us as His children, His "glorious inheritance."

**Action 3.  Believe for God's Power** (know God's "incomparably great power")

Paul's third point in this prayer is in verse 19: that we would know God's "incomparably great power for us who believe. That power is like the working of his mighty strength." This is a power-packed verse — the only verse in the New Testament which contains the three major Greek words for "power": *working, mighty* and *strength.* Paul introduces these words by calling God's power "incomparably great." The Greek for this phrase literally means to "throw an object over a barrier." Paul uses it here to convey that God's power is so great that it goes beyond any limitation or barrier in the universe. God's power is greater than any obstacle in your life.

Paul's first word for power in this verse is the Greek *dunamis,* from which we get our English word *dynamite.* God's power is explosive; nothing can stand in its way. "Working" comes from the same word as the one from which we get *energy.* It means never-ending action. God's incredible, explosive power keeps energizing us day after day to get us past our limitations and change us into the image of Jesus Christ. The other two words, *mighty* and *strength*, also describe God's power.

I think at this point Paul is getting tongue-tied on the subject of God's power. He's exhausted even his

vocabulary defining power, so he continues by describing
how God's power is displayed in the world. God's power
is seen in Christ when . . .

> he [God] raised him [Christ] from the dead and seated him at
> his right hand in the heavenly realms, far above all rule and
> authority, power and dominion, and every title that can be
> given, not only in the present age but also in the age to come.
> And God placed all things under his feet and appointed him
> to be head over everything for the church, which is his body,
> the fullness of him who fills everything in every way (Eph-
> esians 1:20-23).

**First**, God's power is so great that it *raised Christ
from the dead*. That was no mean feat. I think it took
more power to raise Christ from the dead than it did to
create the universe. When God created everything, He
had nothing opposing Him. God just spoke and the universe came into existence (Psalm 33:6-9). When God
raised Christ from the grave, He faced a lot of opposition.
The Roman Empire did everything it could to keep Christ
locked in the tomb. Satan and all his cohorts did all they
could to make sure Jesus stayed dead. Yet God broke the
opposition like you or I snap a toothpick in two.

**Second**, God's power is so great that it *took Christ
into heaven!* Think of the thunderous boosters and tons
of fuel needed to lift the space shuttle and its astronauts
into orbit. Yet God's power lifted Jesus Christ to the
highest heavens without so much as a puff of smoke.

**Third**, God's power is so great that it *placed everything in the universe under the feet of Jesus Christ*. All
authority, power and dominion are under His control.
Every person—including you and me—every problem,
every nation and every planet is under His feet. The entire church is under His authority and rule. You get the
idea from Paul's description that God has a lot of power!

And here's the best news of all: God's great, explosive, never-ending, supreme power is available to everyone who believes in Christ. No matter who you are or

what your background or nationality is, no matter what your limitations may be, God's power is available to help you overcome your past and your problems. No matter what disadvantages you have experienced or are experiencing, God's power is available to change your life. If you have trusted Jesus Christ with your life, you need never again be the victim of your sin, your weakness or your circumstances. You have the greatest power in the universe within you. Tap into this dynamic resource and expect God's power to do great things in your life.

## KEEP ALERT TO DANGER

As you can see from these three guidelines, you have a lot going for you as God's child—but don't let it go to your head. Being proud, self-assured and overconfident is as counterproductive to growth and change as is failing to come to terms with your future, your worth or God's power in your life.

This lesson was brought home to me in a frightening way when I was 28 and still single. At the time I was assistant director of Asian affairs for Campus Crusade for Christ, working with people who were trying to reach university students for Christ. I was near the end of a five-month trip through twenty-seven countries of Asia, Africa and Europe. I had climbed on a plane an average of once every three days during the five months, and by the time I reached my last stop, Manila, I was exhausted.

One evening at dusk, I was walking back to my hotel room when a gorgeous woman appeared from between two buildings. She walked up to me, grabbed my hand and said, "Do you want to have a good time tonight?" I had never talked to a prostitute before. I always thought they were ugly, but this woman was a beauty! I should have pulled away immediately, but I froze.

The woman noticed my hesitancy and took a firmer grip on my arm. "Hey, there's a taxi. Let's go. My husband's not around. We'll have a great time."

You talk about a battle raging inside! I hadn't had a date or an in-depth conversation with a woman for five months. I was tired and lonely, and I wanted a woman to care for me and treat me tenderly. It was the strongest temptation to moral impurity I had ever faced. I knew in my heart that it wouldn't be right, but I was unnerved and immobilized. I couldn't give in, but I couldn't resist.

When the woman tugged me toward the taxi I finally snapped back to reality. "No, I can't," I said just above a whisper. She yanked on my arm again and I blurted out, "I can't go because I know Jesus."

Suddenly she dropped my arm and took two steps back. "Are you a priest?" she demanded, her eyes filled with horror.

"No," I answered, my courage rising, "but I'm a Christian and I know Jesus Christ." Then, with considerably greater courage, I shouted out, "I know Jesus Christ!" The woman was so shocked that she took off running down the street. I returned to my hotel room, and I got down on my knees beside my bed and cried. I had come so close to giving in. No one ever would have known except me — and God.

We walk in a fallen world. Your world is not interested in building you up or strengthening your moral integrity. It will tear you down every chance it gets. Will you let it? Or will you apply God's wealth to your walk and take advantage of God's power for positive change in your life? You must decide to settle your future. You must decide to value your worth. You must decide to believe God for His power in your life. No one else will decide for you. Only as you step *toward* positive changes in these ways will you step *away from* the negative thoughts and behavior which the world, the flesh and the devil beckon you to embrace.

## GUARD YOUR MIND

George had his first sexual experience when he was in high school. That was the beginning. From then on he had one goal in mind for every woman he dated: sex.

In the following months and years, George's life revolved around his sexual conquests. He fed his fantasies by attending sexually explicit movies, listening to music with lyrics which glorified premarital sex, and poring over articles and pictures in skin magazines. Sex was constantly on his mind.

After a couple of years in college, George trusted Christ as his personal Savior. At the time of his conversion George didn't realize all the changes he needed to make in his thought life and his relationships with women. He continued to stock his mind with sexually stimulating materials, and he still planned ways to get the women he dated into bed.

He soon discovered that his sexual exploits as a Christian were followed by a hangover of guilt the next day. He tried to rein in his urges and desires, but his mind was permeated morning, noon and night with thoughts of sex. He knew deep in his heart that God was against his plans to get his dates into bed with him and that he would feel guilty if he carried out those schemes. So George decided to change his ways.

Sometimes, though, his resolve faltered and he went all the way with a date. After each failure he suffered waves of guilt and wondered if he was even a Christian at all. His vacilating lifestyle caused him to doubt the validity of his relationship with Christ. *Will I ever wake up in the morning with a clean mind, a mind which is not cluttered with sexual desires?* George wondered. *Will I ever date a woman without wanting to have sex with her? Is the Christian life always going to be a losing battle with the impure contents of my mind? Will I ever experience the victory that other Christians talk about?*

## THE MIND: A WILD BULL

George's struggle illustrates the great conflict many Christians experience on the road to freedom from sexual regret. The center of the conflict is the mind, and the success of your attempt to live with a clear conscience hinges on the outcome of the battle for your mind.

I look at the human mind as a wild bull. Before you met Christ, your mind roamed freely, thinking what it wanted to think. Like George, you may have provoked your mind to unbridled, impure thoughts by feeding it material which promoted immorality and sexual irresponsibility. Your lifestyle tantalized the raging bull of your mind to dictate your activities with the opposite sex.

When you became a Christian, you discovered, as George did, that the wild bull of your mind was not instantly transformed into a harmless calf. The old thought patterns, ideas, memories and temptations were still there. The wild bull charged recklessly through your nice Christian thoughts and made a shambles of your attempts at purity.

The fact is, you can't turn a wild bull into a house pet. You can put a ring in its nose, though, and lead it out of the house and into a secure pen where it will do the least harm. Similarly, you will never be able to rid your mind totally of all impure thoughts and temptations. Your mind is like a computer with unlimited memory capacity. Every wrong thought, word and deed you have experienced is filed there. It will take a lifetime of spiritual growth, prayer and discipline to smother all that negative input.

In the meantime, the wild bull of your mind snorts and paws the earth, threatening you with thoughts and temptations you wish were gone forever. Thanks to the resurrection power of Christ and the indwelling Holy Spirit, you have the authority to jerk that bull around by the nose and make it behave—but nobody else is going to do it for you. You are the sole guardian of your mind.

Most of the world isn't interested in your desire for a clean mind. Indeed, most of the world will try to invade your mind and manipulate your thoughts. You are being challenged daily to buy certain products, embrace certain ideologies and participate in certain activities. Some of these invitations require you to compromise your standards as a Christian. Somebody must stand at the gate of your mind, regulate what it receives and control its behavior. That somebody is you.

Guarding your mind is a difficult, full-time job, but it's the only way to come to terms with the sexual regrets of your past and move into the freedom of righteousness. I want to share with you several guidelines that will help you guard your mind.

## FILL YOUR MIND WITH TRUTH

Anyone who has worked with computers knows the term GIGO. It's an acronym which stands for "garbage in, garbage out." The phrase reminds the user that if an error shows up in the computer's output, an error was made during input. Good or bad, whatever you put into a computer is what you get out of it.

Just like with the computer, whatever you program into your mind will come out in your behavior. A man came to me once complaining that he couldn't control his sexual urges. "I can't help myself," he concluded. "I'm just oversexed." As I talked with him he admitted that he regularly attended R-rated movies and thoroughly investigated each month's issue of *Playboy*.

"You're not oversexed," I said. "Your activities are trashed up because your mind is trashed up. As long as you keep filling your mind with mental garbage, your behavior will be worldly garbage."

I like to use the term GIGO to stand for "God in, God out." If you want the truth, beauty and purity of God's Word to show up in your behavior, you need to program the truth, beauty and purity of God's Word into your mind. Paul instructed the Philippian Christians:

> Whatever is true, whatever is noble, whatever is right, whatever is pure, whatever is lovely, whatever is admirable — if anything is excellent or praiseworthy — think about such things (Philippians 4:8).

Paul invited believers to flood their minds with positive, godly, scriptural qualities. Only with this kind of input would his readers be able to produce the kind of output he called for in the next verse: "Whatever you have learned or received or heard from me, or seen in me — put it into practice" (Philippians 4:9). Righteous behavior is always preceded by godly thoughts.

The primary reservoir for the positive qualities Paul listed is the Bible. If you want to drown your impure thoughts, you must immerse your mind in God's Word by reading it, studying it, memorizing it and meditating on it. As David said,

> How can a young man keep his way pure? By living according to your word . . . I have hidden your word in my heart that I might not sin against you (Psalm 119:9,11).

John's story illustrates the positive effects of God's Word on the wild bull of an impure mind. John grew up attending church every Sunday. At age twelve he responded to the gospel by receiving Christ as his Savior.

Not long after his conversion, some of John's neighborhood friends introduced him to pornographic magazines. The pictures he saw in those magazines fanned the flames of boyhood lust. Through his junior high and senior high school days John bought his own skin magazines and perpetuated his fascination with pornography. During college he frequented topless bars in an attempt to quench his thirst for tantalizing sights. No matter how much he saw, it never seemed to be enough.

During this time John was also involved in masturbation. He knew his thoughts and lustful desires were wrong, but he felt trapped by his own uncontrollable sexual passions. Shortly after graduating from college he began to realize how miserable he really was. He could see that the path he was traveling was a one-way journey to emotional and spiritual destruction. He desperately wanted inner peace and victory over his obsession with pornography. Finally, he turned back to God, repented of his sins and recommitted his life to Christ.

Unfortunately, John's fierce battle with his impure thought life was far from over. He continued to struggle with lust and the sordid memories from his past involvement with pornography. He found it difficult to resist the temptation to undress in his mind every attractive woman he met. He knew God had forgiven him, but he cried out to God for relief from the dark oppression of his evil thoughts.

The answer came through a new hobby. John joined a Christian band in his home town.

The other members of the band were committed believers who desired to help John mature in his relationship with Christ. One of John's co-workers introduced him to a topical Bible memory system prepared by The Navigators. John began memorizing Bible verses aggressively. Almost immediately the Scriptures which filled John's mind began to transform his thinking about himself, about God and about others.

One of the first verses John committed to memory was 1 Corinthians 6:19,20:

> Do you not know that your body is a temple of the Holy Spirit, who is in you, whom you have received from God? You are not your own; you were bought at a price. Therefore honor God with your body.

John kept this verse card and others lying on top of his desk at work. Whenever an impure thought tempted him, he read or quoted the passage and thought about its meaning in his life. By consciously meditating on Scripture, John diverted his mind from lustful thoughts and focused on positive qualities.

John still struggles with lust and impure thoughts about women, but by saturating his mind with God's Word, he is learning to keep the wild bull in its pen. The Scripture verses John has stored away are gradually helping him overcome the emotional and psychological scars of the past.

George, whose story opened this chapter, had a similar experience. Despite the impurity which seemed to dominate his thinking, George determined to obey God in his behavior. He disciplined himself to read his Bible and pray every day. Soon he realized the importance of memorizing Scripture verses, so he began to do that too.

After a few weeks of memorizing verses, George noticed that he wasn't waking up each morning with thoughts of sex on his mind. Sexual fantasies were occupying less and less of his waking thoughts.

He was able to spend time with a woman on a date and not feel driven to seduce her. It seemed to him that the influx of God's Word through memorization and meditation was cleansing his mind. He began to enjoy the Christian life as the burden of his discouragement over impure thoughts lifted.

As John and George each discovered, victory in the battle for the mind comes through filling your mind with God's truth. The Holy Spirit will use the Bible verses you internalize to transform your mind and your character into the likeness of Jesus Christ. Also, the card file of Scripture verses which you program into your mind will help you replace lustful thoughts with godly thoughts.

Instead of yielding to the temptation of an impure thought, focus your mind on a section of Scripture which answers the temptation. That's how Jesus responded successfully to Satan's temptation (Matthew 4:1-11).

## EXPECT TO BE TEMPTED

Another critical guideline for guarding your mind against future moral failure is to realize that you are not impervious to temptation. Just because you have yielded to the temptation to sexual sin in the past and have received forgiveness doesn't mean you are rendered immune in the future. If anything, you are even more vulnerable. You've been down that road before. Your graphic memories of the experience can amplify the signals of a current temptation. The key to resisting temptation is to be ever alert to its presence and its potential danger.

Temptation can come in many forms. You can be tempted to impure thoughts or behavior by an old flame who calls or shows up at your apartment unexpectedly. You can be tempted by a new acquaintance who is attractive to you. Suddenly you are wondering what it would be like to be intimate with him or her. You can be tempted by the comments of other friends as they discuss their romantic exploits in your hearing. You can be tempted to dwell on illicit relationships promoted in books, magazines, music, TV shows and movies. Even without any outside stimuli, your thoughts and memories can flash tempting scenes on the screen of your mind for you to dwell on.

Remember, temptation is not the same thing as sin. Temptation is an invitation to commit evil. Sin is accepting the invitation. The Bible tells us that Jesus had a perfect record for declining the invitation to sin. He was "tempted in every way, just as we are—yet was without sin" (Hebrews 4:15). You don't need to feel guilty about being tempted. It happens to everyone. Guilt, confession and forgiveness are only necessary when you yield to temptation.

The first target of temptation, and the first area to fall to temptation, is the mind. That's why alertness to temptation is so intrinsic to guarding your mind. A sinful act is always preceded by a sinful thought. Jesus declared that mental adultery is as bad as physical adultery (Matthew 5:27,28). Sin occurs first when your mind accepts temptation's invitation and you commit the act in your imagination. For example, if the memory of a past sexual experience comes to mind, temptation invites you to dwell on that experience, recreate the setting in your mind and willfully relive the encounter. If you are expecting temptation, you can quickly refuse the invitation to mentally commit adultery. When temptation takes your unguarded mind by surprise, you may find yourself well into the mental act before you realize you've fallen.

There are three main contributing elements to every temptation.

The **first** element is *the world with all its alluring temptations.*

The **second** is *your own evil desires.* James wrote, "Each one is tempted when, by his own evil desire, he is dragged away and enticed" (James 1:14).

The **third** element is *Satan,* who "prowls around like a roaring lion looking for someone to devour" (1 Peter 5:8). Satan is actively involved in trying to trip you up. He will bring to mind a romantic experience of the past and tempt you to think on it for awhile. He will tell you that there is nothing wrong with safe, exhilarating sex outside of marriage as long as you love your partner. He will insinuate that God doesn't love you and he will suggest that you fulfill your needs for love and intimacy in physical relationships. Satan always lurks in the shadows, hoping to catch you off guard with his invitations to sin. You can guard your mind against him by being alert to his tricks and refusing his temptations (James 4:7).

## REALIZE YOUR RESOURCES

Another tip for guarding your mind is to be aware of the resources at your disposal for opposing temptation and sin.

**First**, thanks to the victory Jesus Christ won for us in His death and resurrection, neither your evil desires nor Satan can force you to sin. As a Christian, you have *the authority in Christ not to sin.* The Bible says that sin has no more power over you (Romans 6:1-7).

Jesus broke sin's power when He paid its penalty on

the cross and defeated death forever in His resurrection. You are no longer a slave to sin. The choice is yours to refuse the invitations to sin which come from your evil desires and from Satan. Be aware of the potential for victory over temptation which Christ has provided for you.

**Second**, Christ has not only provided you with the authority to say no to sin, but He also has equipped you with *the power to defeat sin*. The indwelling Holy Spirit is present within you to empower you for obedience and righteousness. You cannot resist temptation alone. You need the power of the Holy Spirit flowing through you to guard your mind against sin.

If you find yourself giving in to physical desires or letting your mind entertain impure thoughts that come along, you need to take spiritual inventory to find out what is short-circuiting the Holy Spirit's power in your life. His power is ineffective when you harbor known sin or when you are living for your own desires instead of His. You must confess your sin to God and accept His forgiveness and cleansing. Thank Him that Jesus has already paid the penalty for your sin. Give the Holy Spirit the steering wheel of your life in that area. Let Him guide you out of the danger zones and into His victory.

Through the victory of Christ and the power of the Holy Spirit you have everything you need. Rely on those resources.

## PLAN YOUR DEFENSE

Another important ingredient for guarding your mind against impurity is to prepare your defensive strategies for resisting temptation well in advance. If you wait to plan your defense until you and your partner are snuggled together on the couch in your dimly lit apartment, the battle is already lost. Inflamed passions will always be able to subdue an unguarded mind.

You need to decide long before the event what you will do, how you will respond, and where you will draw the line. If you have a date at 8 P.M., plan your defense against sexual temptation during your morning quiet time with God or at noon while you're eating lunch. That's when you can decide clearly what you will and will not do based on your weaknesses and the temptations you can expect.

For example, let's say that you and your girlfriend are planning to go out to dinner and then return to her apartment to watch a video. You know that everything will be fine unless the two of you lie down on the carpet together to watch the video. That's when your sexual urges start to run wild. Knowing this, don't wait until you get back to her apartment to decide if you will lie down on the carpet. Decide ahead of time that, no matter what happens, you will not lie down with her to watch the video.

You can expect your logical, before-the-fact decisions to be tested in the heat of battle. Your girlfriend may switch on the video and then sprawl on the carpet saying, "Wouldn't you be more comfortable lying here on the floor beside me?" She may turn down the lights and turn up the charm. But if you stick by the decision you made while thinking logically earlier, you will be able to resist the temptation.

If you know that stepping inside her apartment will expose you to more temptation than you can resist, decide in advance to say good-night at the door. If you know that sitting in a parked car for two hours to talk after your date will lead to problems, decide to do your talking at the restaurant, then leave the motor running as you take her to her door.

Anticipate every possibility for failure and mentally lock in a plan of defense or escape.

When it comes to hand-to-hand combat, your passions are stronger than your mind. That's why your mind must outfox your passions by telling them ahead of time what you are going to do. Even when you have made your thoughtful advance decisions, your passions can voice a strong argument at the moment of temptation to alter your plans for purity. Especially be aware of rationalizations such as, "What harm can lying on the floor do?" Prepare yourself for this eventuality by telling a trusted friend of the same sex what you have decided. Ask him or her to pray for you and to call you the next day to ask you pointed questions about your activities with your date.

A good verse for guarding your mind against the temptations to impurity which face you is:

> Clothe yourselves with the Lord Jesus Christ, and do not think about how to gratify the desires of the sinful nature (Romans 13:14).

Your prayerful, logical preparation for temptation will save you countless numbers of problems when the heat is on.

## »»»» STEP 5 «««««

## DISSOLVE IMMORAL RELATIONSHIPS

Frank came to me for counseling concerning his girlfriend Angela. He said she was pulling away from him and he didn't know why. "Frank, tell me about your relationship with Angela," I probed.

"I think we have a pretty good relationship," Frank beamed proudly. "I'm in love with her and I try to show it by being affectionate. In fact, we make love two or three times a month."

I tried to conceal the surprise I felt. "By 'make love,' do you mean that you have sexual intercourse with Angela?" I asked calmly.

"Right," he answered. "We sleep together at her place when her roommate is out of town. Those nights together are really great. That's why I'm so puzzled about Angela's behavior."

"Frank, she is obviously feeling guilty and frustrated," I said. "How can you as a Christian justify premarital sex with Angela?"

"Dick, I love her. Doesn't that make it okay? Why is a little fooling around such a big issue?"

Nick and Tessa were engaged to be married when they came to talk to me. In the course of our discussion about their relationship, they rather sheepishly admitted that they had been sleeping together since they became engaged.

"You're both Christians and you know what the Bible says about premarital sex," I said. "What caused you to start sleeping together before the wedding?"

"We committed ourselves to each other under God when we got engaged," Tessa answered confidently. "The closer we got emotionally, the easier it became to get closer physically. Sure, we feel it might be wrong, but we're already married in God's sight."

## LET'S GET BACK TO THE TRUTH

I hear these weak rationalizations all the time. Some people go to ridiculous lengths to excuse their sinful behavior. Often, they don't want to learn what God's viewpoint is about male/female relationships. From cover to cover in the Bible, the Lord speaks on that topic and He has a lot to say about it. The Scriptures clearly forbid sexual intercourse before marriage, and marriage in the Bible always includes the formal elements of compliance with civil law as well as public acknowledgment.

Furthermore, the Bible doesn't condone sexual activity in couples just because they are engaged. The truth is, almost half of all engaged couples break up anyway.

There is no absolute guarantee that you're going to marry the person you become engaged to. The only valid involvement for sexual activity is within the bounds of legal matrimony.

People today need to accept the truth of God's Word on the issue of sexual relationships. It may sound simple, but it is nonetheless accurate: God knows best. Evaluate your behavior in the light of what the Bible says about healthy relationships, and discipline your mind by aligning it with what He says. If you need to review the facts, earlier chapters in this book spell out in detail God's standards for morality. The "Quotes by God" section, beginning on page 159, contains specific Scripture quotations on the issues of sexual behavior.

One of the greatest gifts you can bring to your eventual marriage is a mind which is disciplined to righteousness by the Scriptures. Everything you say and do is controlled by your mind. Whatever you allow to fill your mind will eventually come out in your behavior. As you endeavor to cleanse your mind with God's Word, righteous behavior will follow.

One of the first responses which should accompany your commitment to God's truth regarding sexual purity is to dissolve all relationships, both present and past, that are pulling your heart and morals away from the Bible's direction for your life.

## LET GOD PURIFY YOUR PAST

Once you allow God's truth regarding moral integrity to discipline your mind, you may feel guilty about impure relationships in your past. Your guilt about that former boyfriend or girlfriend with whom you were sexually active may seem like a blot on your conscience which you desire to clear up. Let me first comfort you and then caution you about dissolving immoral relationships from the past.

First, allow your guilt to prompt you to evaluate

whether or not you have confessed that past sin to God. If you have not, do so now and receive God's forgiveness. Take advantage of God's promise:

> "Come now, let us reason together," says the LORD. "Though your sins are like scarlet, they shall be as white as snow; though they are red as crimson, they shall be like wool" (Isaiah 1:18).

There is great comfort in knowing that God's forgiveness can completely purge your heart of the stains of sin and guilt.

Now for the caution: Don't feel you must go back to an old flame to apologize or ask forgiveness. You may just be sticking your head back into the lion's cage by allowing the confrontation to open old, painful wounds. You may be exposing yourself unnecessarily to a weak spot which could cause you to fall again. I know several people who went to former illicit lovers to apologize, only to fall back into immorality.

The risks of a personal meeting with a former lover are great. The embers of old emotions may unexpectedly flare up and you could get burned. Memories of the good times can subtly overpower your good intentions and you may become vulnerable to a familiar song, a favorite restaurant, etc. You need to know your weak spots and guard against them.

If you feel strongly the need to apologize or seek forgiveness, call that person on the phone instead of visiting him or her in person. If the telephone conversation becomes a temptation to relive former behavior, hang up! Write him or her a letter instead. Don't put yourself in a position where your desire to dissolve an immoral relationship becomes a temptation to resurrect it. It's not worth it.

## BACK OUT OF PRESENT RELATIONSHIPS

This step to freedom from sexual regret may involve even the difficulty of breaking off a present serious relationship which has become immoral.

Let's say that you have recently come to terms with your sexual regret, confessed your sin to God, and accepted His forgiveness. You are rejoicing that the sexual sins of your past are forgiven and forgotten. However, the man you have been sleeping with still wants to be your boyfriend. Or the woman you met, fell in love with, and have been going to bed with is still the woman you want to marry despite your previous failure. The temptations you are fighting now are the same ones you yielded to in the past—and they are just as strong. In addition, this present relationship tends to bring out the worst instead of the best in you. What should you do?

Your first tendency is probably to continue the relationship. After all, you were attracted to the person in the first place, and that attraction may still be strong. You may want to cling to this person because he or she is a tremendous boost to your ego or meets a deep need in your life. Your boyfriend or girlfriend loves you and has been sexually intimate with you. Here is someone who has given himself or herself to you unreservedly, and that makes you feel very special and important. This may be the only person you have ever met who has loved you so deeply. You're remorseful about your sexual sin and you don't want to repeat it—but the thought of this special person walking out of your life is almost too painful to consider.

It may be helpful for you to evaluate your present relationship prayerfully and objectively. The following questions will help you think about the impact of your past and present relationship with this person, especially the sexual intimacy you have shared and may still be sharing:

- Are you being loved or being used?

- In the long run, are you doing a favor or a disfavor to your partner?

- What is the main adhesive in your relationship? Sex or a deeper motive?

- Does your sexual activity distract you from the *person* of your partner or from other important parts of your relationship?

- If your relationship ends, how will having had sex affect the way you view yourself? your partner?

- Does sex cause you to gravitate more and more to one another and to ignore other friends and interests?

- If you end up marrying someone other than your present partner, will the sexual activity in which you are engaging cause you to feel positively or negatively about yourself?

- Will being in a sexual relationship make you feel open and honest or deceitful and secretive in your relationships with your family and friends?[1]

If you want to rid yourself of sexual regret and be free to love again, you have only two choices concerning your present immoral relationships. Both are difficult, but you will never free yourself from sexual regret in your present relationship if you don't make a choice and act upon it. As King Solomon wrote, "Can a man scoop fire into his lap without his clothes being burned? Can a man walk on hot coals without his feet being scorched?" (Proverbs 6:27,28). Trying to live in God's power while retaining the relationship of an old flame is playing with fire.

**Your first choice: Go backward in sharing physical intimacy.**

If you feel you want to institute a morally righteous relationship, you must reverse the progress of your physical involvement. The only way you can do so is to suspend all physical contact with that person — cold turkey — for a minimum of six months. I'm not just talking abstaining from sex. I'm talking about no more skin-on-skin contact whatsoever: holding hands, snuggling in the car or on the couch, kissing — anything.

"Wow, that's pretty radical!" I can hear you saying. "Why must we do something so drastic? Why can't we just back off a little by going part of the way but not all the way?"

Because your habit patterns for physical involvement are already established. You not only know how to get to first base with this individual, sexually speaking, but you know what it means to get to second base, to third base, and to score. You may say, "We'll stop at first base," but once you get to first base, your thoughts and emotions are already programmed from experience to move on to second base and to keep going.

Trying to stop the momentum of lovemaking between two people who have already experienced intercourse is like trying to stop a runaway freight train. You need to make a complete break with those patterns by deciding not to be physically involved with that person. You won't run the bases if you stay in the dugout and refuse to go up to bat.

You will find that suspending all physical activity will help you evaluate the strength of your relationship apart from sex. For example, many couples consider dinner out, a concert, or a movie, as only the preliminaries for the "main event" which happens later in the back seat of the car, on the couch, or in the bed. When you decide to eliminate the main event and that which leads up to it, you're left with the preliminaries — conversation over dinner, watching a movie together, etc. Do you still enjoy being with your partner when the prospect of physical intimacy is out of the picture? Does he or she still enjoy your company? Do you find anything in common beyond a sexual interest in each other? Is there any emotional, intellectual, or spiritual depth to your relationship?

Suspending physical activity will also clarify your partner's motives in the relationship. For example, when you were sexually active, your partner smothered you with, "I'll love you forever"; "I can't live without you"; and, "You're the only one for me." When you tell that person you intend to adopt a lifestyle of moral righteousness and you aren't even going to hold his hand for six months, he may change his tune to: "If I can't make love with you, I'm out of here." You may even discover that what you thought was love was really merely a physical attraction.

Kicking the physical touching habit cold turkey is an extremely difficult step. It requires a complete shift in the basis of the relationship from physical and sexual to spiritual and friendship. In all my years of counseling, I've only known one couple who has successfully taken this step and kept a relationship which led to a healthy marriage. If you don't think your relationship can stand the backward test, you have one other choice to consider.

**Your second choice: Terminate the relationship.**

If you cannot cleanse a present immoral relationship, you must cut the cords and dissolve it. Your commitment to Christ and moral integrity must supersede your commitment to anyone who is a perpetual temptation to moral failure.

Whenever I recommend this serious step to individuals, I try to do so with a measure of hope. I tell them that the separation may not be permanent. God may restore the relationship after a period of separation. That's why I suggest that individuals who separate not destroy the mementos of their relationship: photos, scrapbooks, souvenirs, records or tapes containing "our song," etc. Instead, box them up and store them out of sight until you level off emotionally and discover God's ultimate plan for your relationship.

Craig and Sarah are an encouraging example of what God can do when individuals value personal righteousness above their romantic relationships. Craig was the top football player in our state university when I met him and led him to Christ. He had been sleeping with his girlfriend Sarah on and off for about a year.

As he began studying the Scriptures, he realized that premarital sex was contrary to God's plan for his life. One day he went to Sarah and said, "Sarah, I love you and I want to be with you, but I have recently become a Christian and I can't go to bed with you anymore."

"You're a Christian?" Sarah responded excitedly. "That's wonderful! I'm a Christian too!"

"If you're a Christian, why have you gone to bed with me all these months?" Craig demanded angrily.

"Because I loved you and I wanted you to love me," Sarah answered defensively. "I was afraid that if I didn't give in to you, I would lose you."

When I saw Craig after his confrontation with Sarah he was steamed. He was so deeply repulsed by Sarah's loose behavior as a Christian that he was angry and hostile toward her. I suggested that he break off the relationship and let God heal his wounds. He agreed. Craig wanted nothing to do with Sarah whatever. Because the college they attended was so huge, they were able to avoid each other. They went their separate ways and rarely saw each other, and never spoke.

As the months passed, Craig became a devoted Bible student and his faith in Christ grew remarkably. Unknown to him, Sarah was experiencing a similar growth. The break-up had devastated her, and she responded to her pain by renewing her faith in Christ and committing herself to live a righteous life.

Nearly two years after their separation, Craig and Sarah bumped into each other on campus. They hesitantly shared what God had been doing in their individual lives. Soon they began seeing each other again. They developed an enjoyable friendship based on their mutual commitment to Christ and His guidelines for developing a relationship that will last a lifetime. Two years after their unplanned reunion, Craig and Sarah were married. Today they have three children and a terrific marriage.

Craig and Sarah's story illustrates what God can do when you put Him and His Word above your sexual desires. God used Craig and Sarah's separation in a wonderful way to mature them, purify them, and prepare them for a Christ-centered marriage. They will never forget how God picked up the pieces of their shattered relationship, healed and purified their hearts, and brought them back together.

God may or may not restore a past or present relationship which you dissolve to pursue moral integrity. That's His business. Don't try to determine for God what the future of your relationships should be. You take care of the present decisions by basing your relationships on scriptural guidelines for moral involvement, and then let God take care of the future for both you and your partner. If and when He chooses to bring you back together, it will be wonderful. When God puts people together, He does it right.

## ⟫⟫⟫⟫ STEP 6 ⟪⟪⟪⟪

## PURIFY YOUR PASSIONS

In the last months before they were married, Allison and Darin experienced all the natural romantic, passionate feelings you would expect in two people who were engaged and deeply in love. At that time, Allison was living in Illinois and Darin was living in Colorado. They carried on their courtship mainly through long telephone calls and long letters which were filled with loving words and dreams for the future.

On those sporadic occasions when they did get together, though, their passions were strong and demanding. After being apart for weeks at a time, the tender kisses and embraces were thrilling. They battled against the surging tide of temptation which beckoned them to become sexually involved before reciting their marriage vows. Darin knew he had to keep his sexual urges in check.

He wanted to honor God and show his respect for Allison, but she was so lovable and touchable. He didn't know how to handle his passions during the last weeks before the wedding.

Finally Darin settled on a plan for guiding his behavior when he was alone with Allison. He called it the "Bikini Barrier." Darin told Allison that, until they were married, he would not touch the parts of her body that a bikini would cover. During those long, romantic encounters, when Darin was tempted to explore what would soon be completely his, he remembered his commitment to observe the Bikini Barrier. As a result, Allison's respect for Darin shot sky high, and his decision to keep a tight rein on his passions before the wedding made the honeymoon even more glorious for both of them.

## THE PURITY OF PASSIONS

Like other emotions, passions are amoral. They are neither good nor bad in themselves. There is nothing wrong with passionate feelings. It's your emotional response to your thoughts and circumstances that makes them either a plus or a minus in your relationships with the opposite sex. Like everyone else, you are a romantic, emotional and passionate creature. That's the way God made you. He doesn't want you to ignore or deny the existence of your passions. They are a part of your total makeup. You must learn to bridle your passions and express them in a positive, godly manner.

We often talk about our passions originating in our hearts, but when the Bible talks about passions, it locates them in the area of the solar plexus. The old King James Version of the Bible often referred to inner passions with terms like "bowels of mercies" (Colossians 3:12, KJV) or "bowels of compassion" (1 John 3:17, KJV). Today we say things like, "I have a strong gut feeling"; or, "My stomach is in knots." Our deepest passions affect us physically, in the stomach and the intestines. Sometimes our feelings are so strong that we actually get sick—we can't eat, or our stomach aches. Our passions affect us physically and seem to demand some kind of physical release.

Gut-level human passions are not restricted to romantic feelings or sexual drives. The New Testament describes Jesus Christ as a passionate person, one who felt deeply for the people around Him, but in a nonsexual way. His feelings moved Him to positive responsive action. His passions were channeled to meet the needs of those who stirred His emotions.

He felt compassion for the multitudes so He prayed for them (Matthew 9:35-38), taught them (Mark 6:34), healed their sick (Matthew 14:14), and fed them (Matthew 15:32-38). He was moved to compassion when He met a couple of blind men, and He healed them (Matthew 20:29-34). Jesus' love went out to a leper, and He cured him (Mark 1:40-42). He felt compassion toward the widow of Nain, and He raised her son from the dead (Luke 7:11-17). Jesus always turned feelings of compassion into pure, constructive, positive deeds which served others.

Jesus' emphasis on the greatest commandment reflects His concern that we express our passions in purity in all our relationships:

> "Love the Lord your God with all your heart and with all your soul and with all your mind." This is the first and greatest commandment. And the second is like it: "Love your neighbor as yourself" (Matthew 22:37-39).

More than anything else He taught, Jesus wanted His followers to be totally consumed with love for God and for people. By His example, we know that this all-consuming love was to issue forth in positive, caring deeds. If that's not passion, I don't know what is!

## LIVE FOR YOUR LONGINGS

You can express your passion by wholeheartedly living for your longings. Deep down inside of us we have longings for certain things. These special needs demand to be fulfilled, but satisfying them calls for efforts that are based on understanding their true nature.

What are some of our deep longings? The **first** is a longing for *intimate companionship and friendship*. We desire to deeply love someone, to pour into that person all of the pent-up compassion and caring that fills our heart. We also want to be loved by that person, with equal intensity and honesty. It is a two-way street, giving and receiving.

In my talks I have often said, "What we deeply desire is to be loved for who we really are and to love that person for who they really are. We crave acceptance. No one wants to love a person who is a fake, a superficial pretender. We want to genuinely love and be committed to one person for a lifetime." Thousands have heard that statement and no one has ever said that this was not their deep longing.

The **second** longing we have is for *peace of mind*. The turmoils and stress of daily life hound us. In many ways we are confronted with our weaknesses and limitations. We all desire to be healed of our past sins, which plague our memories, and to experience tranquility in the midst of the pressures of the present.

**Third**, we want *security*. We are often afraid of loneliness, failing, losing at love, rejection and a host of other difficult human emotions. No wonder people will do almost anything to be assured of stability.

**Last**, we long for *significance*. We want to be valuable to somebody, and to know that our life is worthwhile. Regardless of whether we have someone or not, the thought that our life here on this earth counts for nothing is a disheartening one indeed.

The satisfaction of these longings takes time and a set of personal standards that are based on the Word of God. Being single for 42 years of my life, I was able to see how God could satisfy my deep longings. He took away the sting in my life which demanded, "I've *got* to have a woman," and He brought me into building good friendships. It was a strenuous and long process, but God helped me see what my real longings were and kept me from falling for the momentary pleasures.

We all need to develop in our hearts a realization and awareness of our true, deep longings. We also need to expose the things in our life that would detour us from the path of living for those longings. All through life we can expect other cravings and desires to distract us and entice us to get off track. When these times come, we must say emphatically, "No! I'm living for Christ who will fulfill my longings, not for the satisfaction of momentary pleasures." You'll be amazed at the freedom you will enjoy when you can say no to anything that could distract you from your longings. The mixed-up person is the one who can't distinguish his longings from the distractions.

Our society says, "Act responsibly. Be a sexually responsible person." How can we be responsible? Our passions are very strong and can cause us to do things we will eventually regret. That's why you must start with your mind. Your mind says to your passions, "This is the way we're going to go, passions. We are committed to behaving Christ's way." You must decide how you're going to behave long before you get to the place where your passions can steer you off course.

The temptation is always present to short-circuit your deep longings and settle for a momentary pleasure. The reason is simple. It's because those momentary pleasures come, and can be met, in just that amount of time — a moment. Instant gratification wins out over the discipline and time which are required to have your deepest needs met.

In each situation you face you will have a decision to make. Do you live for your longings or for momentary pleasures? Think and pray through this question: "What are my deep longings?" I firmly believe that God, in His way, will satisfy the deepest longings of your heart. Remember this saying:

*"Accept short-term pain to realize long-term gain."*

## KEEPING SEXUAL PASSIONS PURE

Perhaps the most volatile of all human passions are those connected with romantic feelings and sexual urges. Like all our passions, our drives related to the opposite sex need to be expressed in positive, God-honoring ways. Yet we are tempted to let these strong emotions run away with us and dictate our behavior. Sometimes our passion-driven responses toward the opposite sex get us into trouble. In the heat of the moment we are liable to make hasty, selfish decisions we will later regret.

Sexual passions are not wrong, but they do need to be channeled and purified. You need to recognize the power of the drives within you, direct them away from expressions which are immoral and ungodly, and direct them toward expressions which are pure and positive. The Scriptures offer several ways by which you can purify your passions.

### 1. Run from compromising situations.

When your sexual passions start to push you toward moral compromise, you need to purify those passions by getting yourself out of those situations as quickly as possible. Paul instructed the Corinthian Christians, "Flee

from sexual immorality" (1 Corinthians 6:18). He gave a
similar order to Timothy when he wrote: "Flee the evil
desires of youth" (2 Timothy 2:22). To flee literally means
to run for your life. Sometimes you need to purify your
passions by running for your moral life from a tempting
relationship or circumstance.

You can't find a better biblical example of purified
passions than in Joseph, as recorded in Genesis 39:1-12.
As a slave in Egypt, godly Joseph became the faithful servant of Potiphar, the captain of the king's guard. Joseph
was so conscientious in his work that Potiphar gave him
authority over his entire household. Before long, Potiphar's wife began having designs on Joseph's handsome
body. When Potiphar was away, she tempted Joseph to
come to bed with her. Joseph's response to her initial attempts reveals his resolve to subject his passions to God's
authority: "How then could I do such a wicked thing and
sin against God?" (v. 9). Aware of the temptation, Joseph
kept as much distance as possible between himself and
his master's wife.

One day the woman found Joseph alone in the
house. She grabbed Joseph by the cloak and demanded
that he come to bed with her. Joseph didn't stop to argue.
He yanked himself out of her grasp and ran out of the
house, leaving his cloak in her hand. The evil woman was
so upset at Joseph's refusal that she falsely accused him
of assaulting her, using the cloak as evidence against him.
Since Joseph was only a servant, the woman's testimony
was believed and Joseph ended up in prison. God eventually honored Joseph's integrity, though, and used him
to save Egypt, and his own family, from famine.

Joseph's example of moral purity reveals two ways
by which you can flee immorality and purify your passions. **First**, just as Joseph kept his distance from the
tempting seductress, you need to *keep as much space as*

*possible between you and those things which fuel your passions* toward improper responses. For example, if you realize that your sexual desires are aroused by certain books or magazines, don't buy them. If you find yourself wanting to act out with your boyfriend or girlfriend some of the steamy scenes in videos, don't rent those videos. If you can't go into a video store without renting the wrong kinds of movies, don't go into video stores. Become aware of the temptations which pollute your passions and purposely stay away from them.

**Second**, when you find yourself unexpectedly cornered by a potentially compromising situation, *get yourself out of there fast*. Like Joseph, you may become the intended victim of someone else's immoral designs. For example, what do you do when, during a good-night embrace, your boyfriend crosses the Bikini Barrier or your girlfriend urges you toward more intimate sexual contact? Your aroused passions want your date to continue, but you know that in thirty seconds your defenses will crumble and you will be sorry tomorrow. You need to run for your life. Don't try to explain. Just say good-night and leave immediately. You can talk about it later on the telephone, but in the moment of strong temptation your first order of business is to run.

## 2.  Stand strong and resist.

Another method for purifying your passions is to take a biblically defensive stance against temptations to impurity. Paul instructed the Ephesians:

> Be strong in the Lord and in his mighty power. Put on the full armor of God so that you can take your stand against the devil's schemes (Ephesians 6:10,11).

There are times when you need to run from temptation and there are times when you need to stand and fight. If you wanted to escape all human temptation to sexual immorality, you might have to move to a mountaintop to live all by yourself. Even there you would not be outside the realm of temptation because you can't run away from your natural desires, thoughts and memories. You must learn to stand your ground and to defend yourself with the spiritual armor God has provided.

Notice that the first piece of armor Paul lists provided protection for the stomach, intestines and sex organs—the physical counterparts to our inner passions: "Stand firm then, with the belt of truth buckled around your waist" (Ephesians 6:14). For the Roman soldier, the belt was more like a girdle which cinched his free-flowing tunic around his midsection, allowing freedom of movement in battle. Other pieces of armor and weaponry were often attached to the belt, making it an indispensable foundation garment for warfare.

The belt of truth suggests that you must defend your passions against moral compromise with the truth of God's Word. No matter how broadly contemporary society may promote premarital and extramarital sex, the Bible is clear and definite about sex being reserved for marriage. You will be ill-prepared to fend off the world's loose moral standards unless you are firmly grounded in what the Bible says about sex, love and marriage. More personally, you need to "gird up your loins" daily with God's Word in order to make the right decisions when your passions are being tested in relationships with the opposite sex.

## 3. Pursue godly values.

Someone in sports probably coined the phrase, "The best defense is a good offense." That principle is also true in the discipline of purifying your passions. Not only must you defend against sin's encroachment on your passions by fleeing immorality and wearing the armor of truth, but you also must launch an offensive by pursuing positive, godly values.

In the same verse that Paul wrote, "Flee the evil

desires of youth," he added, "and pursue righteousness, faith, love and peace" (2 Timothy 2:22). The word *pursue* in this verse means "to run swiftly in order to catch." It was sometimes used of a bow hunter who had only wounded his prey with his first arrow. As the animal tried frantically to escape its fate, the hopeful hunter relentlessly tracked it, knowing he would eventually outlast his prey and realize his prize.

Paul wrote almost the same instruction to Timothy in his first letter: "Pursue righteousness, godliness, faith, love, endurance and gentleness" (1 Timothy 6:11). In each case, the apostle challenged the young, virile pastor to be relentless in pursuing those positive qualities which would fill his life with the goodness God promises.

Purifying your passions is not just a matter of fending off sin, but also of pursuing righteousness in your whole life. You're not just trying to purge your passions of pollution; you're also trying to infect your passions with godliness, faith, love, peace, etc. Moral purity is not a list of don'ts, it's a discipline of do's.

Pursuing godly values is a difficult process. It just doesn't happen overnight; it takes time. You must discipline yourself to pursue righteousness through prayer, Bible study, making right choices, and saying no to activities of lesser value

It's not an easy life, but then Christ never promised you an easy life. He promised you the best life, and you attain the best life only through the discipline of pursuing goodness. One of the major differences between an Olympic champion runner and the casual neighborhood jogger is persistent hard work and discipline. Christ is calling you to be a champion in the area of purified passions.

## »»»» STEP 7 ««««

## FOCUS YOUR FUTURE

Do you enjoy going to amusement parks? I do. There are all kinds of rides to enjoy, but my all-time favorite is the roller coaster. I don't mind waiting in line to ride one, especially when I can ride either in the front seat or the back seat. I love the front seat of the roller coaster. When I crest that first huge hill and look straight down the steep decline, my heart feels like it's going through the top of my head. When I ride in the back seat I get tossed around so much that it makes my head spin. For me, that's fun!

The roller coaster is full of thrills and chills. An interesting thing about riding the roller coaster, though, is that you go up and down and you get bounced around, but you always end up where you started. You never actually go anywhere. You get lots of excitement, but you make no progress.

The Christian life is not supposed to be a roller-coaster ride. Sure, there are always going to be ups and downs, and sometimes you may get bounced around, but at least you're going somewhere. You're making progress. If your Christian life is like a roller coaster with no progress, you will get discouraged and eventually want to give up the faith.

Similarly, if you're committed to coming to terms with sexual regrets and living a life of moral integrity but just can't seem to make any progress in that direction, you must keep going and stay on the right road. No one wants to get stuck on an endless bumpy ride that goes nowhere. This final step is designed to smooth out some of the hills and valleys of your experience and to produce some discernible progress in your life. When you learn to focus your future, you can step off the roller coaster and really go somewhere with God.

## LEAVE THE PAST BEHIND

Daryl had a tough time getting off the roller coaster of his past sins, especially his sexual activities. He tried repeatedly to get his walk with God going again, but all he did was stumble along making the same mistakes over and over. Daryl wondered if he could ever be free to love again in God's way. Here's how he put it:

I couldn't see how God was going to fulfill in my life Romans 8:28 which promises: "In all things, God works for the good of those who love him." How could he use my past and my sexual involvements with women for good? All I knew was that I had a lot of memories to deal with which were not easy to erase. I was not beyond being tempted again — not by any means. Often I would sit and struggle with my regrets and wish I could relive the past and make better choices.

As I committed myself totally to Jesus Christ

and His lordship in my life, though, I began to
study the Scriptures daily. God's instructions and
promises began to come alive for me. When I read
Paul's words in Philippians 3:13,14, new vigor
and hope began to surge through me. He wrote:
"One thing I do: Forgetting what is behind and
straining toward what is ahead, I press on toward
the goal to win the prize for which God has called
me heavenward in Christ Jesus."

I knew I needed to lay my past sexual failures
at the cross and leave them there. It was time to
press on, to look forward and to concentrate on
all that God wanted me to become.

Now, ten years later, I look back. It's incredible how God has fulfilled His promise to me
to work all things together for good. Through the
years as I have truly sought to know Him, love
Him and, of course, obey Him, He has taken my
past and fulfilled His promise. I have a deeper understanding of people, their needs and why they
choose the course of action they do. God took my
past and used it to help others. He made everything work together for good in my life, something that, in the beginning of my walk with
Him, I never thought He would be able to do.

Daryl learned a principle that we all need to learn
in order to move ahead with Christ: If you want to go forward, you can't look backward. As Paul said, we must forget what is behind and strain toward what is ahead.

It's kind of like a trapeze acrobat in the circus. He
swings back and forth on one bar until another trapeze
bar swings into view. In order to grab onto the new bar
and continue his act, he must let go of the one he's holding onto. He'll never move on to the next phase of his act
until he lets go — and he'll never let go of that bar until
he decides to let go.

Like Daryl, you must let go of your past if you want to move into God's future for your life. The choice is yours. You can continue to allow your past to hinder you or you can accept its lessons and let go of it. You can either wallow in your self-pity and regret over the past or you can reach for and grasp the magnitude of who you are in Christ. You can either remain the pawn of your passions and demanding emotions or you can begin living for your deep longings which will eventually fulfill your heartfelt desires. You can't do both, any more than a trapeze artist can ride two bars at once. You must decide to let go of the past and focus your future, then go for it.

Deciding to focus your future requires another trait displayed by the man on the flying trapeze: faith. When the acrobat lets go of his trapeze, he does so believing that, when he spins around in mid-air, another swinging trapeze bar will be within his grasp. He confidently releases what he can see to reach for something he cannot see, knowing it will be there when he needs it.

Hebrews 11:6 is crystal clear about the importance of faith in following Christ: "Without faith it is impossible to please God." Faith focuses on the God who is above the circumstances of life. It sees His invisible characteristics flowing in and through the person who trusts the Lord. If all you ever do is deal with the things and circumstances you can see, you will be like everyone else—depending solely on self to get by. That's just a long, bumpy roller-coaster ride going nowhere. On the other hand, faith touches the supernatural power of God, the movement of the Lord in everyday events in which you are involved. When you learn to tap into the unseen godly dimension by faith, you will experience a unique power to face the future, and you'll never be the same.

## DEVELOP INTIMACY WITH GOD

As I mentioned in Step 6, Jesus Christ summarized

the essence of our focus in life when He declared that the greatest of all commandments is to love God intimately (Matthew 22:37). It's interesting that Christ's statement is a direct quote from the Old Testament. Loving God is not just a New Testament idea; God has always wanted us to love Him intimately. He doesn't choose favorites, but He does desire intimates. He wants each of us to be intimate with Him. If you focus your life and your future on developing a loving, intimate relationship with God, you're in tune with what the Scriptures say. To know God intimately is the greatest goal in life. As you focus on that goal, everything that detracts from it will become unimportant by comparison.

Developing an intimate relationship with God does not happen overnight. It's a never-ending, lifelong process which involves persistent study of the Scriptures and prayer. Becoming intimate with God also means inviting Him into every area of your life and making Him the focus of everything you do. Loving God is a daily commitment which requires discipline, perseverance and determination. Yet the joy of the journey is fantastic, especially when you take advantage of God's promise of strength:

> The LORD . . . gives strength to the weary and increases the power of the weak. Even youths grow tired and weary, and young men stumble and fall; but those who hope in the LORD will renew their strength. They will soar on wings like eagles; they will run and not be weary, they will walk and not be faint (Isaiah 40:28-31).

## REACH OUT TO OTHERS

According to Christ, the second greatest commandment is to love people (Matthew 22:39). To fulfill His command we need to focus on reaching out to others in love despite our feelings of pain, depression or discouragement. Reaching out to others even when I don't feel like it is one of the lessons I learned while still single. Whenever I was hurt because of a broken relationship, I was tempted to withdraw from people to soak and sour in loneliness and self-pity.

One day my thoughts were jolted. It seemed God was saying to me, "Dick, you're responding to your pain in the wrong way. Don't withdraw from people when you're hurting; reach out to them. Don't center on your pain; center on hope. Don't be a stagnant pond with no outlet; be a flowing river of love and concern to others."

I discovered that focusing on others instead of myself was the key to restoration from my own pain. The more I reached out to others, the less time and energy I had to feel sorry for myself.

Sometimes it's hard to love others who don't love us in return or who reject us or cause us pain. We're tempted to turn away from them because they turned away from us, but can you imagine what would have happened if Jesus had responded to His hurt by withdrawing? He might have said, "Nobody appreciates Me. Everybody has rejected Me. Do you think I'm going to get hurt again by going to the cross? Forget it." Thank God, He didn't do that! Instead, He kept reaching out to people until His death on the cross touched the whole world with God's love. When people cause us pain, we need to forgive them the same way Jesus did: "Father, forgive them, for they do not know what they are doing" (Luke 23:34).

In the midst of your hurt you still have something to offer another person, even if it's just a listening ear. As you listen, you will discover you are not alone in your pain. Others are suffering too and you can minister to them from what you have learned. Second Corinthians 1:3-7 instructs us to comfort others with the comfort we have received from God. God heals us so that we can help others to heal. Listen to them and share with them what God has done for you. It will be healing to your soul as you reach out and comfort others.

## LEARN TO SAY NO

Another way to focus your future is by learning to say no to anything which would sidetrack you from your goals. In the secular culture, saying no to sexual pleasure is disdained because it means holding back on your fun or setting aside a good-time experience. Instead, our culture urges us to satisfy our cravings and do what feels good. If you follow that advice, pretty soon you're going every which way but not getting anywhere, doing everything but accomplishing nothing.

We need to say no to some things. In fact, you ought to stand in front of the mirror every day and practice saying, "No, no, no, no, no." Then, when a questionable activity or relationship begs you to say yes, you will be well practiced to decline it. Here are a few examples:

**Say no to people who tear you down.**

In Step 5, I said that if you are involved in a relationship with the opposite sex which is eroding your moral integrity, you need to say no to that relationship. "But," you may object, "if I break up with her, she'll be hurt."

Perhaps, but by continuing the relationship you are being decimated. Don't try to protect the other person at the expense of your own future. Also, don't try to play God in that person's life. Do what you must do to honor Christ and leave the other person in God's hands.

Others resist saying no to a damaging relationship by rationalizing, "If I break off with him, he'll never come to Christ because I'm the only Christian he knows."

That's like telling the Holy Spirit He can't reach your friend without your help. You not only have a relationship problem, you have a faith problem. You don't believe in the power of God. You need to trust the Holy Spirit to reach your friend even if you leave the relationship.

Saying no to a relationship is not the end of the world, although it may feel like it for awhile. During my years as a single adult, I was involved in broken romantic relationships with many different women. Some of them were casual dating relationships and others were more serious. Even though none of them were immoral, five of those breakups were tragic to me—heartbreaking. Still, it was through those hard times that I learned some great lessons about myself, love, friendship and trusting God. If you let God teach you to say no to the relationships He says no to, you will be richer for it.

## Say no to lesser things.

I love to read the newspaper. Some days I'll spend a long time reading a paper and put off talking to God and reading the Bible. When I get to the end of the day I say, "Sorry, God, I didn't have time to meet with You today." Then as I look back on my day, I realize I would have been better off meeting with God for an hour and skipping some of the newspaper. I said no to the greater thing and yes to the lesser thing.

There is nothing wrong with reading newspapers or good books, watching TV, going shopping, etc., but if these things detract from the things that really help your life stay on track, you must say no to them. There's an old saying which goes something like, "The good is the enemy of the best." Sometimes our lives are missing the best because we have not learned to say no to the good.

## Say no to time pressures.

Don't allow yourself to get frazzled by pressures in your daily time schedule. We all seem to be caught up in a whirlwind of activities. Somebody says, "Let's go for pizza"; or, "Let's play basketball"; or, "Let's go to a movie." You don't want to turn your friends down or miss out on a good time, but your calendar is overloaded. You're missing out on needed rest; you're not doing a good job at work; you're lagging in your personal time with God. Learn to bring coordination to your life and say no to things that tend to knock your life out of balance.

## KEEP YOUR WOUNDS IN PERSPECTIVE

As intent as you are to forget your past and focus on your future, you may still be smarting from emotional and spiritual wounds resulting from your sin. It is important to keep your wounds in perspective — God's perspective. Being free to love again requires being able to see why those wounds are there. I believe there are four reasons God allows our wounds to remain.

**First**, our wounds *drive us to Christ,* the Wounded Healer. To repeat what I said earlier, God's purpose in our lives is to work everything out for good so that we are conformed to the image of Christ (Romans 8:28,29).

Sometimes, though, when things are not going too smoothly, we forget God's purpose for us and we fail to cooperate with His goal of making us like Christ. If we didn't have wounds, we wouldn't need God and we'd go straight to hell — but when we're hurting, we come running back to God. Have you ever noticed that you pray more when things are going wrong? I thank God for the wounds still in my life. Yes, my sins have produced some of those wounds, but the consequences of those sins drove me to God and all things are working together for His good in my life.

**Second**, our wounds *drive us to each other.* Wounded people need each other. If we didn't hurt, we wouldn't need each other, and we would be the loneliest creatures on earth. Instead, our wounds drive us to each other for comfort, counseling, encouragement and help.

**Third**, our wounds *make us more sensitive* to other wounded people. If you ever have been deeply hurt in a relationship, or have gotten involved in things that were wrong, and God has brought you out of them, you're more sensitive to others in a similar boat. Furthermore, you have learned to accept God's forgiveness, forgive yourself, guard your mind, dissolve immoral relationships, etc. You're equipped with compassion and experience to help someone who's struggling in this area.

**Fourth**, our wounds *glorify God*. Christ and His disciples approached a blind man and His disciples asked, "Who sinned, this man or his parents, that he was born blind?" (John 9:2). Jesus said that the man's blindness wasn't his fault or his parents' fault. Instead, it was an occasion through which God would be glorified.

Sometimes we don't know why we have wounds. We ask God, "Why this? Why me? Why now?" but we don't seem to get an answer. My only comfort is to know that God will use my wounds to glorify Himself. I don't understand what Jesus meant by His statement, but I can trust that He knows what He's doing even when I don't.

My little daughter Rachel came to me once and asked, "Daddy, can we have a horse?" Our backyard at the time was so small that the sprinkler hit all four corners when I set it in the middle of the yard. But Rachel, in her childish innocence, wanted to put a horse back there.

I could have railed on her for her stupid idea. I could have recited all the logical reasons: The yard is too small; the law doesn't allow horses in our city; we can't afford to board a horse, etc. However, although she was a child and was unable to understand my reasons, I still wanted her to keep coming to me with her desires and questions. So I simply said, "Rachel, I love you and I would love to give you a horse, but we just can't have one in our yard. You can keep asking me for other things, though."

I think God is the same way. We may not understand

the whys of our wounds, but we know that the God who understands the whys loves us and invites us to keep seeking Him and His ways.

## CHOOSE RIGHTEOUSNESS

Moses grew up with the privileges and prestige of Egyptian royalty. Opulence and wealth surrounded him. Egypt was the foremost military and political power in the world and Moses was the adopted son of the king's daughter. He could have had it all: fame, fortune, women, power. Instead, Moses chose to serve God:

> He chose to be mistreated along with the people of God rather than to enjoy the pleasures of sin for a short time. He regarded disgrace for the sake of Christ as of greater value than the treasures of Egypt, because he was looking ahead to his reward (Hebrews 11:25,26).

Instead of identifying with the royal family, Moses opted to be called a Hebrew slave and seek God's righteous ways. Did he make a dumb choice? History tells us the story. He is considered one of the greatest leaders of all time. And, although we don't fully know what God's reward to Moses was, God did select Moses to appear with Elijah on the Mount of Transfiguration when Jesus was on earth (Mark 9:2-4).

Focusing your future means choosing righteousness above all other choices and leaving the rewards to God. Serving God with moral integrity may cost you some fleshly pleasure and desirable relationships, but ultimately, you will not be sorry for choosing God's ways over the desires of your flesh. The pleasures of sin look good, but the results are always negative in the long run. In contrast, when you focus your future on God's righteousness, God promises some tremendous blessings and benefits. Here's a small sampling from Psalms:

- The Lord watches over your way (1:6).
- The Lord surrounds you with His favor (5:12).

- The Lord is present with you (14:5).

- The Lord sees you and hears your prayers (34:15).

- The Lord delivers you out of your troubles (34:19).

- The Lord condemns your foes (34:21).

- The Lord upholds you (37:17).

- The Lord refuses to forsake you (37:25).

- The Lord becomes your stronghold in troubled times (37:39).

- The Lord sustains your life (55:22).

- The Lord shines His light on you (97:11).

- The Lord loves you (146:8).

Choosing righteousness is not a dumb choice. It's the only smart choice. God's rewards are worth enduring any momentary discomfort you may suffer from the world, the flesh or the devil.

## CHOOSE OBEDIENCE

God asked Moses to leave the security of his Egyptian family and accept a new identity, a new role and a new mission. Did Moses have a choice? Of course he did. God never forces us to obey Him. He invites us to choose obedience to Him and promises His presence and provision as we do so. Focusing your future means committing yourself unreservedly to obeying God in your life.

Sometimes obedience to God carries a high price tag. Moses lost his security, his wealth, his friends, his prestige, his power—everything. He was probably ridiculed, laughed at, called derogatory names, rejected and humiliated for his choice. Yet he paid the price because of His commitment to obey God: "By faith he left Egypt, not fearing the king's anger; he persevered because he saw him who is invisible" (Hebrews 11:27). Moses' focus was on his future and the unseen God who would guide him through it. God calls us to make the same choice.

I don't know a better illustration of a couple committing their lives and futures to God than the story of Tom and Sharon. They fell in love while working in the same city during summer vacation. They both returned to college in the fall; Tom to Dallas and Sharon to St. Louis. During the school year they wrote romantic letters to each other. Being apart was hard on both of them. They wanted very much to be together.

At the same time Sharon was being tormented by a growing dilemma. She sensed God was guiding her to become a missionary to Indonesia. The more she prayed and the more she read the Bible, the more her heart went out to the people there who needed Christ. Whenever she read anything about Southeast Asia, she was thrilled at the possibility of taking God's message of love there.

Sharon hadn't talked to Tom about Indonesia. Sure, they had discussed some of their plans for after graduation, but she had kept quiet about what God was saying to her about missionary service.

Thanksgiving weekend was approaching. Tom was coming to visit and Sharon was confused. She loved him deeply, but she didn't know if he would want to serve Christ with her in Indonesia. What if she decided to follow Christ's leading and Tom didn't want to go? She wondered if he had become more important to her than God.

When Tom arrived, Sharon was excited to see him, but she was so upset inside she couldn't bear to tell him about her dilemma. That first night they attended a lecture by a missionary from Asia. The room was so crowded when they arrived that they could not sit together. So Sharon sat in the chair directly in front of Tom.

As the missionary spoke, she prayed, "Lord, speak to Tom. Show him Your purpose for his life—and show me Your purpose for mine."

Sharon could not mistake the moving of the Lord in her heart. When the missionary spoke about Indonesia, her mind was filled with possibilities of going there—but what about Tom? What was he thinking? What was God saying to his heart? Sharon knew that she must choose to follow God's leading regardless of God's plan for Tom. In the stillness of her heart, she affirmed her commitment to serve God in Indonesia—with or without Tom.

After the meeting, Sharon turned her chair around. "Well, what do you think about everything you heard?" she asked cautiously. He was silent for only a moment, but it seemed like ten years to her. "I really haven't said much to you about the specific direction of my future," he began, "but tonight confirmed it in my heart."

"Oh, Tom, what is it?" she asked breathlessly.

"I really love you, Sharon. You are very important to me—but the Lord is directing me to become a missionary to Indonesia." Sharon almost fell off her chair with shock and excitement.

Tom and Sharon have loved God and each other for more than thirty-three years. They have served the Lord together with their three children in various parts of the world, including thirteen years in Indonesia.

Tom and Sharon demonstrate to me and countless others the rewards of focusing our future on Christ and His plan for our lives. He knows you, He knows your future, He knows your mate or, if your are to get married some day, he knows all about your future mate and his or her future. When you give everything you are and have to Him, your future will be in clear focus.

# »»»» EPILOGUE ««««

## YOU CAN DO IT!

Do you feel overwhelmed? After reading the Steps to Freedom and all the suggestions to help you restore your life and move forward, you may think that the task is beyond your abilities and strength. Cheer up; it is!

That's where faith comes in. Only Christ can change your life. Only He can completely transform your attitudes and behavior. In and of yourself, you cannot be what God wants you to be. Only God can bring about the permanent changes in you which will please Him. The apostle Paul put it this way:

I can do everything through him who gives me strength (Philippians 4:13).

Recently I received this hope-filled letter from Bill:

*Remember me? I talked with you a year ago after you spoke at a meeting I attended in my city.*

*I shared with you my struggle with giving away my virginity.*

*I had sex only once, but I was overwhelmed with the reality of what I had given up and how fundamentally wrong my actions were. Every time I heard someone speak about premarital sex and its destructive effects, I felt like I was being torn apart inside.*

[Tears came to my eyes.]

*You told me that you were planning to write a book on the exact topic I needed to hear about. You encouraged me to study God's Word, pray and write to you if I found any Scriptures that were particularly helpful. Well, I've found my "regeneration verse." It's 2 Corinthians 5:17: "Therefore, if anyone is in Christ, he is a new creation; the old has gone, the new has come!" Dick, I realized and continue to realize that through accepting Christ's death on the cross as payment for my sin, I have been made new, and I continue to be made new every day. I can never become a physical virgin again, but since my mind, body and spirit have been renewed, Christ has allowed me to become a spiritual virgin again. I cannot give my future wife my virginity in a physical sense, but I can do so spiritually and emotionally.*

*It has taken several years and a lot of God's working, but I have come a long way. I have dated several women who have been very supportive, and God has used them tremendously to help me deal with all this.*

You also are a new creation if you have given your life to the Lord Jesus Christ. Trust Him day by day for the power to be changed into the righteous person He wants you to be. Yes, it will be tough for you in this corrupt world. The temptations are still there. Your Pandora's box has been opened and the negative stuff is still hitting you. Your passions sometimes act like a hungry lion ready to leap out of the cage and attack.

But wait a minute. Remember, God has slammed the lid shut and you have hope. Christ has put a new spirit of life inside you. The Holy Spirit is your constant indwelling companion ready to empower you for battle. In Him is your victory. Believe it!

Even though Marion had received Christ as a child, she had been wild and rebellious ever since she could remember. During her high school and college years she was deeply involved in drugs, alcohol and partying. Life was boring to Marion, so she welcomed anything that might bring her some excitement. She found that drugs did not keep her high long enough, though, and there was always that awful letdown. She tried to fill the void with boyfriends and parties. The despair only grew worse. She was tired of living and afraid to die.

One of Marion's neighbors, a Christian woman named Anna, saw Marion's painful struggle. As they talked one day, Anna said, "Marion, why don't you get your life together? Come back to Christ and really let Him be the Lord of your life."

"Oh, I've tried many times to do that, but I always fail," she responded. "I can't do it."

"Yes, you can."

"No, I can't."

"Yes, you can."

"No, I can't."

"Yes, you can."

"Do you really believe I can?" Marion asked with a

deep sigh.

"Yes," Anna said confidently, "Jesus Christ wants you to come to Him, seek His forgiveness and trust Him for His power to change your life."

Marion's faith was so weak that she didn't think God could do anything good in her life. She had treated Him so badly for so many years. She did realize, though, that Anna believed in Christ's power to change her life, so Marion stepped out on Anna's faith. "I will try it because you believe God can work in my life. Some day I hope to grow in my own faith."

Marion took the Steps to Freedom. The verses that gave her personal confidence were 2 Corinthians 12:9,10:

> He said to me, "My grace is sufficient for you, for my power is made perfect in weakness." Therefore I will boast all the more gladly about my weaknesses, so that Christ's power may rest on me. That is why, for Christ's sake, I delight in weaknesses, in insults, in hardships, in persecutions, in difficulties. For when I am weak, then I am strong.

It has been more than fifteen years since Marion set out on her renewed journey with Christ. She's had many ups and downs, but Christ has smoothed them out and has given her courage to change her habits to please Him. She is now happily married to a godly man and has two lively children.

How about you? Do you believe Christ can restore your purity and joy? Do you believe you can be free to love again?

If you have a hard time believing it, go on my faith. You can do it!

# »»»» APPENDIX «««««

## QUOTES BY GOD

Do you want to know exactly what God thinks about a specific topic? He has put His ideas and thoughts on paper, and it is called the Bible.

It is vitally important that we make sure our thoughts and behavior are in line with His clear statements. When you think and live according to His will, you will experience His rewards and His blessings.

These "Quotes by God" give you passages on four topics covered in this book. Study the verses often and meditate on their meaning. Ask God to apply them to your life. Memorize several passages in each category so you will have them in your mind when temptations hit you or when doubts come.

When I was a young boy, I learned a little saying that has carried me through many rough waters:

*"God said it; I believe it; and that settles it."*

So fill your mind and your life with the Word of God. Thank Him for His promises. They are yours to rely upon.

>>>>>  ¤  <<<<<

## QUOTES BY GOD

## Sex Outside Marriage

### EXODUS 20:14

"You shall not commit adultery."

### PROVERBS 2:16-22

[Wisdom] will save you also from the adulteress, from the wayward wife with her seductive words, who has left the partner of her youth and ignored the covenant she made before God. For her house leads down to death and her paths to the spirits of the dead. None who go to her return or attain the paths of life.

Thus you will walk in the ways of good men and keep to the paths of the righteous. For the upright will live in the land, and the blameless will remain in it; but the wicked will be cut off from the land, and the unfaithful will be torn from it.

### PROVERBS 5:1-23

My son, pay attention to my wisdom, listen well to my words of insight, that you may maintain discretion and your lips may preserve knowledge. For the lips of an adulteress drip honey, and her speech is smoother than oil; but in the end she is bitter as gall, sharp as a double-edged sword. Her feet go down to death; her steps lead straight to the grave. She gives no thought to the way of life; her paths are crooked, but she knows it not.

Now then, my sons, listen to me; do not turn aside from what I say. Keep to a path far from her, do not go near the door of her house, lest you give your best strength to others and your years to one who is cruel, lest strangers feast on your wealth and your toil enrich another man's house. At the end of your life you will groan, when your flesh and body are spent. You will say, "How I hated discipline! How my heart spurned correction! I would not obey my teachers or listen to my instructors. I have come to the brink of utter ruin in the midst of the whole assembly."

Drink water from your own cistern, running water from your own well. Should your springs overflow in the streets, your streams of water in the public squares? Let them be yours alone, never to be shared with strangers. May your fountain be blessed, and may you rejoice in the wife of your youth. A loving doe, a graceful deer — may her breasts satisfy you always, may you ever be captivated by her love. Why be captivated, my son, by an adulteress? Why embrace the bosom of another man's wife?

For a man's ways are in full view of the LORD, and he examines all his paths. The evil deeds of a wicked man ensnare him; the cords of his sin hold him fast. He will die for lack of discipline, led astray by his own great folly.

## PROVERBS 6:23-35

These commands are a lamp, this teaching is a light, and the corrections of discipline are the way to life, keeping you from the immoral woman, from the smooth tongue of the wayward wife. Do not lust in your heart after her beauty or let her captivate you with her eyes, for the prostitute reduces you to a loaf of bread, and the adulteress preys upon your very life. Can a man scoop fire into his lap without his clothes being burned? Can a man walk on hot coals without his feet being scorched? So is he who sleeps with another man's wife; no one who touches her will go unpunished.

Men do not despise a thief if he steals to satisfy his hunger when he is starving. Yet if he is caught, he must pay sevenfold, though it costs him all the wealth of his house. But a man who commits adultery lacks judgment; whoever does so destroys himself. Blows and disgrace are his lot, and his shame will never be wiped away; for jealousy arouses a husband's fury, and he will show no mercy when he takes revenge. He will not accept any compensation; he will refuse the bribe, however great it is.

## 1 CORINTHIANS 5:9-11

I have written you in my letter not to associate with sexually immoral people — not at all meaning the people of this world who are immoral, or the greedy and swindlers, or idolaters. In that case you would have to leave this world. But now I am writing you that you must not associate with anyone who calls himself a brother but is sexually immoral or greedy, an idolater or a slanderer, a drunkard or a swindler. With such a man do not even eat.

## EPHESIANS 5:3-7

Among you there must not be even a hint of sexual immorality, or of any kind of impurity, or of greed, because these are improper for God's holy people. Nor should there be obscenity, foolish talk or coarse joking, which are out of place, but rather thanksgiving. For of this you can be sure: No immoral, impure or greedy person—such a man is an idolater—has any inheritance in the kingdom of Christ and of God. Let no one deceive you with empty words, for because of such things God's wrath comes on those who are disobedient. Therefore do not be partners with them.

## ROMANS 13:12-14

The night is nearly over; the day is almost here. So let us put aside the deeds of darkness and put on the armor of light. Let us behave decently, as in the daytime, not in orgies and drunkenness, not in sexual immorality and debauchery, not in dissension and jealousy. Rather, clothe yourselves with the Lord Jesus Christ, and do not think about how to gratify the desires of the sinful nature.

## 1 THESSALONIANS 4:3-8

It is God's will that you should be sanctified: that you should avoid sexual immorality; that each of you should learn to control his own body in a way that is holy and honorable, not in passionate lust like the heathen, who do not know God; and that in this matter no one should wrong his brother or take advantage of him. The Lord will punish men for all such sins, as we have already told you and warned you. For God did not call us to be impure, but to live a holy life. Therefore, he who rejects this instruction does not reject man but God, who gives you his Holy Spirit.

## MATTHEW 5:27-30

You have heard that it was said, "Do not commit adultery." But I tell you that anyone who looks at a woman lustfully has already committed adultery with her in his heart. If your right eye causes you to sin, gouge it out and throw it away. It is better for you to lose one part of your body than for your whole body to be thrown into hell. And if your right hand causes you to sin, cut it off and throw it away. It is better for you to lose one part of your body than for your whole body to go into hell.

## 1 CORINTHIANS 6:13-20

"Food for the stomach and the stomach for food"—but God will destroy them both. The body is not meant for sexual immorality, but for the Lord, and the Lord for the body. By his power God raised the Lord from the dead, and he will raise us also. Do you not know that your bodies are members of Christ himself? Shall I then take the members of Christ and unite them with a prostitute? Never! Do you not know that he who unites himself with a prostitute is one with her in body? For it is said, "The two will become one flesh." But he who unites himself with the Lord is one with him in spirit.

Flee from sexual immorality. All other sins a man commits are outside his body, but he who sins sexually sins against his own body. Do you not know that your body is a temple of the Holy Spirit, who is in you, whom you have received from God? You are not your own; you were bought at a price. Therefore honor God with your body.

## REVELATION 21:6-8

He said to me: "It is done. I am the Alpha and the Omega, the Beginning and the End. To him who is thirsty I will give to drink without cost from the spring of the water of life. He who overcomes will inherit all this, and I will be his God and he will be my son. But the cowardly, the unbelieving, the vile, the murderers, the sexually immoral, those who practice magic arts, the idolaters and all liars—their place will be in the fiery lake of burning sulfur. This is the second death."

## REVELATION 22:13-16

I am the Alpha and the Omega, the First and the Last, the Beginning and the End.

Blessed are those who wash their robes, that they may have the right to the tree of life and may go through the gates into the city. Outside are the dogs, those who practice magic arts, the sexually immoral, the murderers, the idolaters and everyone who loves and practices falsehood.

I, Jesus, have sent my angel to give you this testimony for the churches. I am the Root and the Offspring of David, and the bright Morning Star.

## Forgiveness and Restoration

### PSALM 51:1-12

Have mercy on me, O God, according to your unfailing love; according to your great compassion blot out my transgressions. Wash away all my iniquity and cleanse me from my sin.

For I know my transgressions, and my sin is always before me. Against you, you only, have I sinned and done what is evil in your sight, so that you are proved right when you speak and justified when you judge. Surely I was sinful at birth, sinful from the time my mother conceived me. Surely you desire truth in the inner parts; you teach me wisdom in the inmost place.

Cleanse me with hyssop, and I will be clean; wash me, and I will be whiter than snow. Let me hear joy and gladness; let the bones you have crushed rejoice. Hide your face from my sins and blot out all my iniquity.

Create in me a pure heart, O God, and renew a steadfast spirit within me. Do not cast me from your presence or take your Holy Spirit from me. Restore to me the joy of your salvation and grant me a willing spirit, to sustain me.

### PSALM 103:12

As far as the east is from the west, so far has he removed our transgressions from us.

### HEBREWS 10:15-17

The Holy Spirit also testifies to us about this [one sacrifice]. First he says:

"This is the covenant I will make with them after that time, says the Lord. I will put my laws in their hearts, and I will write them on their minds."

Then he adds:

"Their sins and lawless acts I will remember no more."

### 1 JOHN 1:7-9

If we walk in the light, as he is in the light, we have fellowship with one another, and the blood of Jesus, his Son, purifies us from all sin.

If we claim to be without sin, we deceive ourselves and the truth is not in us. If we confess our sins, he is faithful and just and will forgive us our sins and purify us from all unrighteousness.

## COLOSSIANS 2:13,14

When you were dead in your sins and in the uncircumcision of your sinful nature, God made you alive with Christ. He forgave us all our sins, having canceled the written code, with its regulations, that was against us and that stood opposed to us; he took it away, nailing it to the cross.

## EPHESIANS 1:3,4

Praise be to the God and Father of our Lord Jesus Christ, who has blessed us in the heavenly realms with every spiritual blessing in Christ.

## EPHESIANS 2:1-10

As for you, you were dead in your transgressions and sins, in which you used to live when you followed the ways of this world and of the ruler of the kingdom of the air, the spirit who is now at work in those who are disobedient. All of us also lived among them at one time, gratifying the cravings of our sinful nature and following its desires and thoughts. Like the rest, we were by nature objects of wrath.

But because of his great love for us, God, who is rich in mercy, made us alive with Christ even when we were dead in transgressions — it is by grace you have been saved. And God raised us up with Christ and seated us with him in the heavenly realms in Christ Jesus, in order that in the coming ages he might show the incomparable riches of his grace, expressed in his kindness to us in Christ Jesus.

For it is by grace you have been saved, through faith — and this not from yourselves, it is the gift of God — not by works, so that no one can boast. For we are God's workmanship, created in Christ Jesus to do good works, which God prepared in advance for us to do.

## ISAIAH 1:18

"Come now, let us reason together," says the LORD. "Though your sins are like scarlet, they shall be as white as snow; though they are red as crimson, they shall be like wool."

## 1 CORINTHIANS 6:9-11

Do you not know that the wicked will not inherit the kingdom of God? Do not be deceived: Neither the sexually immoral nor idolaters nor adulterers nor male prostitutes nor homosexual offenders nor thieves nor the greedy nor drunkards nor slanderers nor swindlers will inherit the kingdom of God. And that is what some of you were. But you were washed, you were sanctified, you were justified in the name of the Lord Jesus Christ and by the Spirit of our God.

### 2 CORINTHIANS 5:17

Therefore, if anyone is in Christ, he is a new creation; the old has gone, the new has come!

### ROMANS 6:22,23

Now that you have been set free from sin and have become slaves to God, the benefit you reap leads to holiness, and the result is eternal life. For the wages of sin is death, but the gift of God is eternal life in Christ Jesus our Lord.

## Rewards Of Righteousness

### GALATIANS 5:16-25

So I say, live by the Spirit, and you will not gratify the desires of the sinful nature. For the sinful nature desires what is contrary to the Spirit, and the Spirit what is contrary to the sinful nature. They are in conflict with each other, so that you do not do what you want. But if you are led by the Spirit, you are not under law.

The acts of the sinful nature are obvious: sexual immorality, impurity and debauchery; idolatry and witchcraft; hatred, discord, jealousy, fits of rage, selfish ambition, dissensions, factions and envy; drunkenness, orgies, and the like. I warn you, as I did before, that those who live like this will not inherit the kingdom of God.

But the fruit of the Spirit is love, joy, peace, patience, kindness, goodness, faithfulness, gentleness and self-control. Against such things there is no law. Those who belong to Christ Jesus have crucified the sinful nature with its passions and desires. Since we live by the Spirit, let us keep in step with the Spirit.

### PSALM 1:1-3

Blessed is the man who does not walk in the counsel of the wicked or stand in the way of sinners or sit in the seat of mockers. But his delight is in the law of the LORD, and on his law he meditates day and night. He is like a tree planted by streams of water, which yields its fruit in season and whose leaf does not wither. Whatever he does prospers.

## PSALM 37:27-31

Turn from evil and do good; then you will dwell in the land forever. For the LORD loves the just and will not forsake his faithful ones.

They will be protected forever, but the offspring of the wicked will be cut off; the righteous will inherit the land and dwell in it forever.

The mouth of the righteous man utters wisdom, and his tongue speaks what is just. The law of his God is in his heart; his feet do not slip.

## PSALM 92:12-15

The righteous will flourish like a palm tree, they will grow like a cedar of Lebanon; planted in the house of the LORD, they will flourish in the courts of our God. They will still bear fruit in old age, they will stay fresh and green, proclaiming, "The LORD is upright; he is my Rock, and there is no wickedness in him."

## PSALM 112:1-9

Praise the LORD.

Blessed is the man who fears the LORD, who finds great delight in his commands.

His children will be mighty in the land; the generation of the upright will be blessed. Wealth and riches are in his house, and his righteousness endures forever. Even in darkness light dawns for the upright, for the gracious and compassionate and righteous man. Good will come to him who is generous and lends freely, who conducts his affairs with justice. Surely he will never be shaken; a righteous man will be remembered forever. He will have no fear of bad news; his heart is steadfast, trusting in the LORD. His heart is secure, he will have no fear; in the end he will look in triumph on his foes. He has scattered abroad his gifts to the poor, his righteousness endures forever; his horn will be lifted high in honor.

## PROVERBS 11:30

The fruit of the righteous is a tree of life, and he who wins souls is wise.

### PROVERBS 14:34

Righteousness exalts a nation, but sin is a disgrace to any people.

### JEREMIAH 17:7-10

"Blessed is the man who trusts in the LORD, whose confidence is in him. He will be like a tree planted by the water that sends out its roots by the stream. It does not fear when heat comes; its leaves are always green. It has no worries in a year of drought and never fails to bear fruit."

The heart is deceitful above all things and beyond cure. Who can understand it?

"I the LORD search the heart and examine the mind, to reward a man according to his conduct, according to what his deeds deserve."

### ROMANS 8:12-17

Brothers, we have an obligation—but it is not to the sinful nature, to live according to it. For if you live acccording to the sinful nature, you will die; but if by the Spirit you put to death the misdeeds of the body, you will live, because those who are led by the Spirit of God are sons of God. For you did not receive a spirit that makes you a slave again to fear, but you received the Spirit of sonship. And by him we cry, "*Abba,* Father." The Spirit himself testifies with our spirit that we are God's children. Now if we are children, then we are heirs—heirs of God and co-heirs with Christ, if indeed we share in his sufferings in order that we may also share in his glory.

### 2 CORINTHIANS 4:16-18

Therefore we do not lose heart. Though outwardly we are wasting away, yet inwardly we are being renewed day by day. For our light and momentary troubles are achieving for us an eternal glory that far outweighs them all. So we fix our eyes not on what is seen, but on what is unseen. For what is seen is temporary, but what is unseen is eternal.

### REVELATION 2:7

He who has an ear, let him hear what the Spirit says to the churches. To him who overcomes, I will give the right to eat from the tree of life, which is in the paradise of God.

## MATTHEW 5:3-12

Blessed are the poor in spirit, for theirs is the kingdom of heaven. Blessed are those who mourn, for they will be comforted. Blessed are the meek, for they will inherit the earth. Blessed are those who hunger and thirst for righteousness, for they will be filled. Blessed are the merciful, for they will be shown mercy. Blessed are the pure in heart, for they will see God. Blessed are the peacemakers, for they will be called sons of God. Blessed are those who are persecuted because of righteousness, for theirs is the kingdom of heaven.

Blessed are you when people insult you, persecute you and falsely say all kinds of evil against you because of me. Rejoice and be glad, because great is your reward in heaven, for in the same way they persecuted the prophets who were before you.

# Overcoming Temptation

## 1 CORINTHIANS 10:12,13

So, if you think you are standing firm, be careful that you don't fall! No temptation has seized you except what is common to man. And God is faithful; he will not let you be tempted beyond what you can bear. But when you are tempted, he will also provide a way out so that you can stand up under it.

## 1 PETER 5:6-9

Humble yourselves, therefore, under God's mighty hand, that he may lift you up in due time. Cast all your anxiety on him because he cares for you.

Be self-controlled and alert. Your enemy the devil prowls around like a roaring lion looking for someone to devour. Resist him, standing firm in the faith, because you know that your brothers throughout the world are undergoing the same kind of sufferings.

## EPHESIANS 6:10-18

Be strong in the Lord and in his mighty power. Put on the full armor of God so that you can take your stand against the devil's schemes. For our struggle is not against flesh and blood, but against the rulers, against the authorities, against the powers of this dark world and against the spiritual forces of evil in the heavenly realms. Therefore put on the full armor of God, so that when the day of evil comes, you may be able to stand your ground, and after you have done everything, to stand. Stand firm then, with the belt of truth buckled around your waist, with the breastplate of righteousness in place, and with your feet fitted with the readiness that comes from the gospel of peace. In addition to all this, take up the shield of faith, with which you can extinguish all the flaming arrows of the evil one. Take the helmet of salvation and the sword of the Spirit, which is the word of God. And pray in the Spirit on all occasions with all kinds of prayers and requests. With this in mind, be alert and always keep on praying for all the saints.

### 2 PETER 1:3-9

His divine power has given us everything we need for life and godliness through our knowledge of him who called us by his own glory and goodness. Through these he has given us his very great and precious promises, so that through them you may participate in the divine nature and escape the corruption in the world caused by evil desires.

For this very reason, make every effort to add to your faith goodness; and to goodness, knowledge; and to knowledge, self-control; and to self-control, perseverance; and to perseverance, godliness; and to godliness, brotherly kindness; and to brotherly kindness, love. For if you possess these qualities in increasing measure, they will keep you from being ineffective and unproductive in your knowledge of our Lord Jesus Christ. But if anyone does not have them, he is nearsighted and blind, and has forgotten that he has been cleansed from his past sins.

### 1 JOHN 2:15-17

Do not love the world or anything in the world. If anyone loves the world, the love of the Father is not in him. For everything in the world—the cravings of sinful man, the lust of his eyes and the boasting of what he has and does—comes not from the Father but from the world. The world and its desires pass away, but the man who does the will of God lives forever.

### JAMES 4:7,8

Submit yourselves, then, to God. Resist the devil, and he will flee from you. Come near to God and he will come near to you. Wash your hands, you sinners, and purify your hearts, you double-minded.

## TITUS 2:11-14

The grace of God that brings salvation has appeared to all men. It teaches us to say "No" to ungodliness and worldly passions, and to live self-controlled, upright and godly lives in this present age, while we wait for the blessed hope—the glorious appearing of our great God and Savior, Jesus Christ, who gave himself for us to redeem us from all wickedness and to purify for himself a people that are his very own, eager to do what is good.

## PHILIPPIANS 4:8,9

Finally, brothers, whatever is true, whatever is noble, whatever is right, whatever is pure, whatever is lovely, whatever is admirable—if anything is excellent or praiseworthy—think about such things. Whatever you have learned or received or heard from me, or seen in me—put it into practice. And the God of peace will be with you.

## PSALM 139:23,24

Search me, O God, and know my heart; test me and know my anxious thoughts. See if there is any offensive way in me, and lead me in the way everlasting.

## COLOSSIANS 3:1-10

Since, then, you have been raised with Christ, set your hearts on things above, where Christ is seated at the right hand of God. Set your minds on things above, not on earthly things. For you died, and your life is now hidden with Christ in God. When Christ, who is your life, appears, then you also will appear with him in glory.

Put to death, therefore, whatever belongs to your earthly nature: sexual immorality, impurity, lust, evil desires and greed, which is idolatry. Because of these, the wrath of God is coming. You used to walk in these ways, in the life you once lived. But now you must rid yourselves of all such things as these: anger, rage, malice, slander, and filthy language from your lips. Do not lie to each other, since you have taken off your old self with its practices and have put on the new self, which is being renewed in knowledge in the image of its Creator.

## HEBREWS 12:1-3

Since we are surrounded by such a great cloud of witnesses, let us throw off everything that hinders and the sin that so easily entangles, and let us run with perseverance the race marked out for us. Let us fix our eyes on Jesus, the author and perfecter of our faith, who for the joy set before him endured the cross, scorning its shame, and sat down at the right hand of the throne of God. Consider him who endured such opposition from sinful men, so that you will not grow weary and lose heart.

# »»»» REFERENCE NOTES ««««

**Chapter One**

1. Michael Gibson, *Gods, Men and Monsters From the Greek Myths* (New York, NY: Schochen Books, 1982).

**Chapter Three**

1. Linda Wolfe, "The New Sexual Realism," *Ladies' Home Journal* (April 1987).

**Chapter Four**

1. Randy C. Alcorn, *Christians in the Wake of the Sexual Revolution* (Portland, OR: Multnomah Press, 1985).

2. Ben Stein, *The View From Sunset Boulevard* (New York, NY: Doubleday and Co., 1980).

3. Robert Lichter, Stanley Roghtman, et al, "Hollywood and America: The Odd Couple," *Public Opinion* (December/January, 1983).

**Step 1.**

1. Don Baker, *Beyond Choice: The Abortion Story No One Is Telling* (Portland, OR: Multnomah Press, 1985).

2. Josh McDowell, *The Secret of Loving* (San Bernardino, CA: Here's Life Publishers, 1985).

3. Les Carter, *Mind Over Emotions* (Grand Rapids, MI: Baker Bk. Hse., 1985).

**Step 5**

1. Adapted from Michael Cavanaugh, *The Effective Minister* (San Francisco, CA: Harper & Row, 1986).

# ABOUT THE AUTHOR

Dick Purnell is the founder and director of Single Life Resources, a ministry of Campus Crusade for Christ. In addition, he is an internationally known speaker and author.

A graduate of Wheaton College, Dick holds a Master of Divinity degree from Trinity Evangelical Divinity School and a master's degree in education (specializing in counseling) from Indiana University.

Dick is the author of *Becoming a Friend and Lover*, *Building a Relationship That Lasts*, and the *31-Day Experiment* series.

Dick and his wife Paula have two daughters, Rachel and Ashley. They love living in North Carolina.